Inspired by Flowers

25 BEAUTIFUL
NEEDLECRAFT PROJECTS

Inspired by Flowers

25 BEAUTIFUL
NEEDLECRAFT PROJECTS

Caroline Green and Di Lewis

David & Charles

A DAVID & CHARLES BOOK

ISBN 0 7153 0004 0

Printed in Italy by LEGO SpA
for David & Charles
Brunel House Newton Abbot Devon

Contents

Introduction

The first stirrings of the idea for this book started several years ago
when Di Lewis and I first met. She had been commissioned to
photograph some of the craft work that I had done
for various women's magazines and eventually we met on a
photographic session. I knew and admired the natural flair she had for
her photography, particularly with flowers,
and I was thrilled with the delightful mood that her pictures
gave even the simplest of my designs.
Over the years we worked together many times on small and large
projects, and, on one rather miserable February day,
waiting for the rain to stop, we decided that the time had come to
bring out a book of our own.
Flowers seemed the obvious choice as a subject, and I decided to make
something different to go with each type of flower.
Thus this book shows some of my favourite techniques,
all inspired by our most loved flowers.

Lavender
bedroom accessories

Most people think of lavender flowers as a distinct bluey mauve, but I was surprised to find that lavender comes in many different shades, from almost white, through pink and pale mauve to deepest purple. The foliage varies too in different tones of grey-green. I looked at the flowers closely and decided that the best way to represent them was in simple embroidery stitches. I designed a corner motif that can be used singly for a dressing table tray or tissue box, or in twos or fours to adorn a larger cloth, and a single lavender stem can be used to form a border design.

Lavender flowers can be used fresh or dried in arrangements and look best with a few sprigs tied together in small bunches. A simple arrangement of lavender stems cut to one length and pushed evenly into styrofoam is most effective. This can then be displayed in small terracotta flower pots, baskets or any unusual container.

Above: To dry lavender flowers successfully, the stems should be picked just before the tiny flowers come out. Tie them into small bundles and hang them in a warm room for a few weeks until the stems are brittle. Push them, in clumps, into unusual containers like these little metal buckets, for a long lasting wall decoration.

Materials for the embroidery

- 50cm(½yd) white DMC Salamanca fabric 3945
- Approximately 2 skeins each, DMC stranded cotton (floss) 3364, 341, 340, 3746, and 554
- Crewel embroidery needles
- Embroidery frame (optional)
- White sewing cotton
- Fine black waterproof felt-tipped pen
- Soluble embroidery marker pen
- Tracing paper
- 14 x 20cm(5½ x 8in) white card or thin perspex for tray
- 30.5 x 24cm(12 x 9½in) Bondaweb fusible fleece
- Narrow satin ribbon
- Square box of tissues
- Small towel
- Toning bias binding, 2.5cm(1in) wide
- Narrow elastic
- Bodkin

Right: Embroidering lazy daisy stitch in shades of mauve and violet is the perfect way to represent lavender flowers. Choose a finely woven fabric on which to stitch and then make up the pieces into delightful dressing table accessories.

To make the tray

1. Trace the lavender pattern onto tracing paper, using the black felt-tipped pen (Fig 1).

2. Cut out a piece of linen measuring 30.5 x 24cm(12 x 9½in) for the tray. Place this over the traced pattern so that the lavender motif is placed centrally, 5.5cm(2¼in) from the short left-hand edge. Pin the pattern in place and, using the soluble marker pen, draw in the lines of the design onto the fabric.

3. Use three strands of stranded cotton (floss) for the stitching. Cut it into pieces about 50cm(20in) long to avoid tangling as you sew. You can work in an embroidery frame if you wish.

4. Following the lazy-daisy-stitch diagram (Fig 2), begin by stitching the tiny lavender flowers in shades of light and dark mauve. Shade the colours on each stem using the photographs on page 9 as a guide.

5. Next embroider the stems in stem stitch (Fig 3) using the green stranded cotton (floss). Then embroider the ribbons in pink and mauve, the outlines in stem stitch and across the ribbon with satin stitch (Fig 4).

6. Use a brush dipped in clean water to remove any lines from the traced design. Press the back of the stitching carefully before making it up. Lay the embroidered fabric face down onto a piece of clean cotton cloth. Lay another piece of cotton on top and press gently with a steam iron. This method raises the texture of the stitches rather than flattening and distorting them.

7. Cut out another piece of the fabric and a piece of Bondaweb to the same size as the embroidered piece. Cut a piece of white card or perspex to measure 14 x 20cm(5½ x 8in). (If you use perspex you will be able to wash the tray later without damaging it.) Iron the Bondaweb onto the plain fabric and peel off the backing paper when it has cooled. Lay the perspex centrally onto this and then the embroidered piece on top. Press round the edge with a fairly hot iron to bond the layers together. Now stitch close to the perspex with white thread to hold it in place.

8. Using a small glass and a pencil, draw rounded corners onto the fabric and then trim to shape. Bind all around the edge with the contrasting bias binding. Stitch pairs of snap fasteners or short pieces of ribbon 5cm(2in) from either side of each corner. Join these to pull up the sides and form the tray (Fig 5).

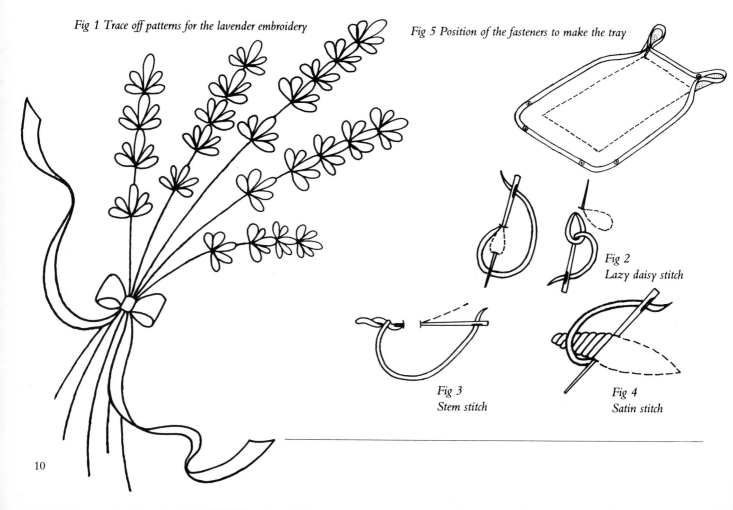

Fig 1 Trace off patterns for the lavender embroidery

Fig 5 Position of the fasteners to make the tray

Fig 2 Lazy daisy stitch

Fig 3 Stem stitch

Fig 4 Satin stitch

To make the tissue-box cover

1. Cut out a 50cm(20in) square of the fabric. Cut this in half. Using the soluble marker pen, trace the lavender motif onto the pieces of fabric so that it is placed centrally, 7.5cm(3in) from the lower edge. This will make the embroidery fall on opposite sides of the tissue box.

2. Follow the embroidery instructions for the tray.

3. Using the bias binding, bind the top, long raw edge of the embroidered pieces of fabric. Place the pieces together, with the binding touching. Use ladder stitch to join them, leaving a 6.5cm(2½in) gap in the middle of the seam to pull the tissues through.

4. With the wrong side of the fabric uppermost, place the fabric centrally over the tissue box so that the opening will allow the tissues to be pulled through. Hold it in position, with pins pushed into the corners of the box, and then pin the side seams so that the cover fits (Fig 6). Remove the fabric carefully and machine stitch the four side seams. Trim the seams close to the stitching and press open.

5. Turn under a 2.5cm(1in) hem along the raw edge of the cover and stitch to make a channel. Insert some elastic into the channel and pull the cover onto the box. Pull up the elastic to hold the cover in place, then tie the ends and trim off neatly.

To make the towel

1. Following the embroidery instructions for the tray, stitch single lavender stems onto a strip of the fabric about 8cm(3in) wide and slightly longer than the width of your towel.

2. When complete turn under the edges of the fabric and machine stitch across the towel. Add stitched-on lines of narrow satin ribbon or binding to complete.

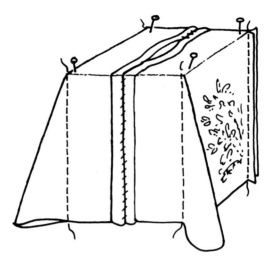

Fig 6
Stitching the tissue-box cover side seams

Lavender mixed with selected leaves and petals makes a wonderfully perfumed pot pourri.

Sunflower

covered boxes, books and frames

In Europe, sunflowers are grown as crops in the fields,
thousands of giant blooms lifting their faces to the sun, en masse.
As well as their size, it is the colour and textural qualities of sunflowers
that particularly attract me. So, for the items in this chapter I have chosen
richly patterned fabrics and paper to decorate a selection of frames, boxes,
books and files to brighten up the dullest work area.
In gardens, we tend to grow just a few sunflowers at a time as a splash of
colour, and a dramatic change of height. It's interesting to see just how
tall they can grow – children love to watch them and compete for the
tallest plant. As cut flowers, they are best kept to large dramatic displays
where their rich golden yellow stands out like a beacon.

Materials

- Patterned furnishing fabrics
- Silk in toning colours
- Giftwrap or posters of sunflowers
- PVA glue and spreader for paper
- Copydex glue for fabric
- Satin ribbon
- 56g(2oz) polyester wadding
- Various boxes, frames and books to cover
- Varnish

Left: Bring the warmth of summer sunshine into your rooms with these fabric-and-paper-covered accessories in sunflower shades.

Right: Mix exotic strelitzia flowers with sunflowers and variegated foliage to make a stunning display in an empty fireplace.

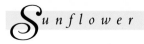

To make the frame

1. Remove all the backing card and glass from the frame. Using scrap paper, cut a strip the width of the flat area on each side of the frame, ready to cut out the sunflower paper. Lay the paper strip over one side of the frame, hold it in place and carefully cut along both mitres with a craft knife (Fig 1). Make sure this is accurate. For a rectangular frame, make another template for the longer or shorter side.

2. Lay these templates onto the back of the sunflower paper and draw round them. Cut out and try each piece in position on the frame. Trim if necessary and then spread the back of each piece with PVA glue. Press each piece in place, pushing out any air bubbles.

3. When the glue is dry, brush on several coats of varnish, leaving it to dry between coats. Re-assemble the frame with the chosen picture.

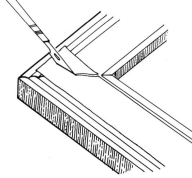

Fig 1 Cut the mitres on the paper patterns

To cover the square box

Whatever the size or shape of your chosen box, the basic method for covering it will be the same. Concentrate on the outside surfaces first, folding the excess paper or fabric to the inside and then decorate the interior of the box to complete.

1. First cut a piece of paper that will go round the lower half of the box, overlapping slightly at the back and with excess paper at the top and bottom (Fig 2). Using PVA, glue this in place, snipping the excess paper at the corners so that it will fold over the edges of the box neatly.

2. Cut an oversize piece of paper for the top of the box lid. Glue it in place, snipping and folding over the excess paper onto the sides of the lid (Fig 3). Cut a strip of paper for the sides of the lid. Glue it on so that the edge will run along flush with the top of the lid and the lower part will fold onto the inside.

3. Varnish the outside of the box and leave it to dry. Lastly, neaten the box base with a slightly smaller square of paper or felt to protect the furniture.

4. Decorate the inside of the box by covering thin pieces of card with contrasting paper or fabric and gluing them neatly inside, one by one.

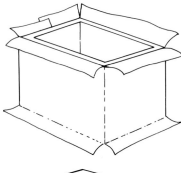

Fig 2 Glue the paper round the box, with excess top and bottom

Fig 3 Cover the top of the box lid and fold the excess paper to the sides

Left: A heart-shaped jewel box and diary covered in silk would make a delightful gift for a favourite friend.

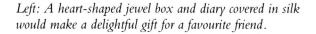

To cover the heart-shaped box

1. First cut a piece of fabric on the cross, that will go round the lower half of the box, overlapping slightly at the back and with excess at the top and bottom. Glue this round the box base, snipping into the excess fabric at the top and bottom edge. Fold these tabs over and glue in place to neaten.

2. Cut out a piece of wadding to fit the top of the lid. Cut an oversize piece of fabric and lay it over the top. Pulling the fabric taut, glue it in place, snipping and folding over the excess fabric onto the sides of the lid.

3. Cut a strip of paper to fit the sides of the lid. Cover this with an oversize piece of the fabric. Fold the top edge of fabric to the back of the card, and then glue the covered piece onto the lid so that the top edge will run along flush with the top of the lid and the lower part of the fabric will fold onto the inside (Fig 4).

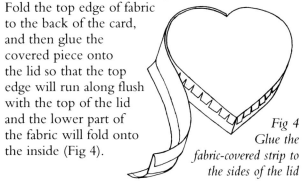

Fig 4
Glue the fabric-covered strip to the sides of the lid

4. To decorate the top of the lid, cover a 7.5cm(3in) diameter circle of card with wadding and contrasting fabric, gluing the excess fabric to the back. Cover a piece of piping cord with a strip of fabric cut on the cross. Glue this to the back of the covered circle so that it fits round the edge. Now glue the padded circle to the top of the box. This can be purely decorative or you can use it as a pincushion.

5. Decorate the inside of the box by covering thin pieces of card with contrasting fabric and gluing them neatly inside, one by one. You can pad these with wadding if you like. Lastly, neaten the box base with a slightly smaller piece of felt.

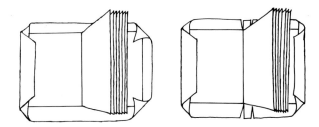

Figs 5 and 6
Pull the points of paper diagonally over the corners, then glue the side edges. Snip into the paper at the spine

A sheet of wrapping paper, printed with a painting of sunflowers, was the inspiration for this easy transformation of a simple wooden frame.

To cover books and files

1. Lay the book open flat onto the reverse side of the paper or fabric you are going to cover it with. Cut out the covering, adding about 5cm(2in) all round. Spread glue over the front cover of the book and press the covering smoothly in place.

2. Open the book and fold the corners of the covering to the inside, pulling the points diagonally across the corners (Fig 5). Glue in place. Now glue the side edge of the covering to the inside of the front cover. Repeat this process with the back cover.

3. Snip into the excess covering along the top and bottom of the book at the points where the covers join the spine (Fig 6). Tuck the resulting tabs of covering to the inside of the spine and glue in place.

4. Now fold the top and bottom edges of covering to the inside of the cover and glue.

5. Decorate the corners of the book by gluing on pieces of ribbon or contrasting paper triangles at this stage. Fold and glue the excess to the inside covers as before. Add a ribbon book mark glued inside the top of the spine.

6. Spread glue over the first and last page of the book and then close the book carefully so that the edges of the covering on the inside of the book are concealed. On a file simply glue on a sheet of decorative paper, cut to size, for the same effect.

Snowdrop
cutwork window blind

The snowdrop design has been machine-embroidered onto the edge of white, moiré-patterned fabric to decorate the window blind.
When the stitching is complete, parts of the fabric are carefully snipped away to leave a shaped edge and a cutwork effect. The design has been stitched in a lovely soft, grey-green to match the colour of the snowdrop leaves. This border can be used for the edge of a simple roller blind or a pleated Roman blind.
These crystal wine glasses and Victorian glass custard dishes, arranged with antique bottles on a wide country-house window ledge, make a delightful and practical setting for fresh snowdrops.
Their delicate stems need to be supported in small vessels of water, and the window forms a natural frame, allowing the flowers to be lit by shafts of spring sunshine. Stand one saucer-shaped wine glass inside another to give height to the composition and arrange mounds of rich green moss with some trailing foliage to complete the design.

You will need to make up this simple roller blind with a double fabric border at the lower edge, below the lath channel. This should measure about 15cm(6in) deep, to accommodate the cutwork embroidery.

Materials

- A roller blind kit to fit your window recess
- Bondaweb fusible fleece to fit across the width of the blind, 15cm(6in) wide
- Fabric to fit your window (see overleaf)
- Spray fabric stiffener
- Staple gun or hammer and tacks
- Tracing paper
- Fine waterproof felt-tipped pen
- Dressmaker's carbon paper
- Masking tape
- Several reels of pale green sewing thread
- Sharp, pointed needlework scissors

Left: This tiny, moss-covered basket is the perfect container for a handful of snowdrops. Push a small jar inside the basket, to hold water and then decorate around it with clumps of dampened moss and trailing leaves to create a woodland atmosphere.

Right: The pretty window blind has a repeating, Art Nouveau style, snowdrop motif.

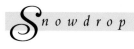

1. Measure your window recess carefully and mark the fabric to exactly the right width and add 30cm(12in) to the length. It is very important that the fabric is exactly square so that the blind rolls up and down straight. Cut the top and bottom edges. Fold up the lower edge of the fabric 18cm(7in) on the wrong side and press the fold. Lay the Bondaweb inside the fold and iron in place . Pull off the backing paper and iron so that the two layers are bonded together. Stitch a channel across the blind, through both layers of fabric so that it fits the lath for the bottom of the blind (Fig 1).

2. Work on the blind before it is stapled to the roller and with the lath removed. Trace the snowdrop design onto the tracing paper (Fig 2). Tape the tracing near the edge of the border so that the centre line on the design is exactly in the centre of the blind and the lower points are about 2.5cm(1in) from the fold. Slip the carbon paper under the tracing, shiny side down, then follow the lines of the design with a hard pencil or a ballpoint pen to transfer the shapes onto the fabric. Be careful not to smudge the carbon on the fabric where it may show later.

Fig 1 Iron on Bondaweb to hold up the lower edge of the blind, then stitch the channel for the lath

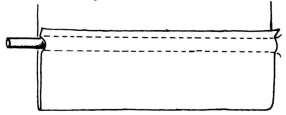

When you have completed this area lift the tracing and replace it further along the blind, matching up the pattern. Continue in this way until the design reaches the edges of the blind. Adjust the ends of the design, if necessary, so that the pattern ends in a convenient place.

3. Thread up your sewing machine with the green thread. Adjust it to a very close-set zigzag stitch so that the end result looks like satin stitch. Make the stitch width very slightly wider than the lines on the snowdrop pattern. This will ensure that you cover the coloured lines. Use a spare piece of the blind fabric to try out the stitching before you begin on the finished blind.

This close-up picture of the cutwork embroidery shows the very close-set zigzag stitching that gives the look of satin stitch. The width of the stitch is graduated as you work, to make the points and shaped areas.

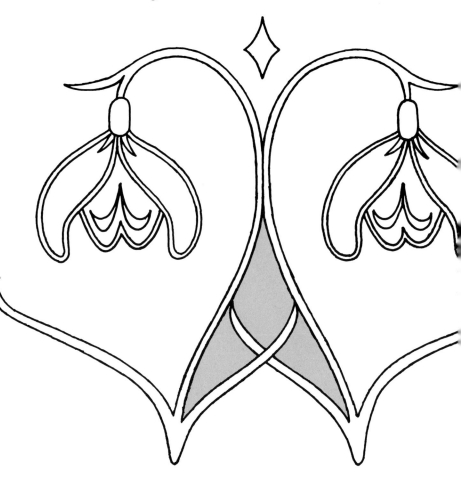

4. When you are happy with your stitching, start by working the snowdrop flowers, then the stems and lastly the leaves. If you work in this order, the ends of each row of stitching will be neatly covered by the next row and thus avoid lots of ends to finish off by hand. As you sew, use the stitch width adjustment to form the points so that you follow the design exactly.

5. When you have finished the stitching, turn the work over and use the point of a pin to pull all the loose thread ends to the back. Tie these in pairs and trim off neatly. Some threads will have been stitched into the work and you can trim these off close to the embroidery.

6. Using the needlework scissors, carefully cut away the shaded areas on the pattern between the stems. Cut as close to the stitching as you can without cutting any of the threads. If you do cut a thread by accident, secure it quickly with a tiny dab of PVA glue, before any stitching comes undone. Next cut out the lower edge of the border in the same way, to complete the design (Fig 3).

7. Using the staple gun, or hammer and tacks, attach the top of the blind to the roller. Make sure it will hang level and stretch the fabric slightly as you attach it to avoid creases. Hang the blind up temporarily, preferably out of doors and spray with the fabric stiffener, following the maker's instructions. Pay particular attentionto the side edges to prevent the fabric from fraying as the blind is being used. You may need to re-cut these edges to get a really straight line, after the stiffener has dried. Then insert the lath in the channel and hang the blind up at the window, using the fixings provided with the kit.

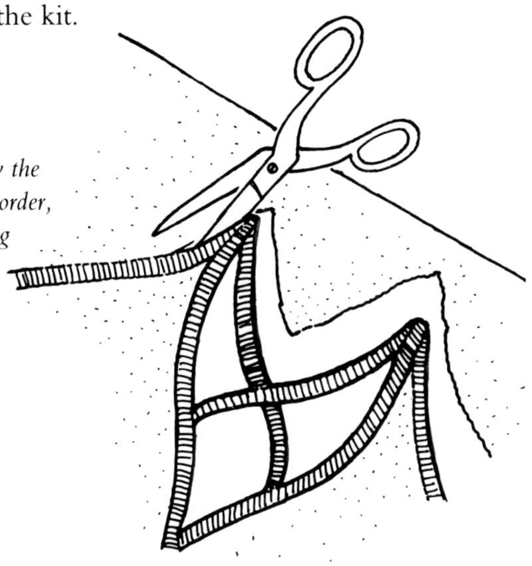

Fig 3
Carefully cut away the lower edge of the border, close to the stitching

Fig 2
Full-size pattern for the snowdrop motif

Bluebell
appliqué mirror frame and collar

There's nothing quite like the heavenly colour of a wood filled with a carpet of bluebells as far as the eye can see. The magical purpley-blue contrasts beautifully with the new leaves just bursting out on the trees, and the delicious scent of flowers fills the whole wood. The shape and colour of a single bloom inspired me to make this simple appliqué design and I have used it to decorate a white collar and a padded fabric mirror frame. Both projects are quite quick and easy to make with a trace-off shape to follow. I have added painted detail to each flower but this is not absolutely necessary if you are unsure about your painting skills.

Mirror frame

Materials

- Scraps of lightweight silk in about five shades of blue
- 46cm(18in) square of plain white silk
- 7.5 x 64cm(3 x 25in) blue silk for bow
- 46cm(18in) square of thick polyester wadding
- Bondaweb fusible fleece
- 18.5cm(7¼in) diameter round mirror
- Sheet of thick white card
- Thin card for backing
- Thin paper for patterns
- Pair of compasses
- Ruler
- Craft knife
- Masking tape
- Fine black waterproof felt-tipped pen
- Small sharp scissors
- PVA glue
- Setacolour fabric paints in parma violet and white
- Fine watercolour brush

Left: The mirror frame is made from circles of card, padded and then covered with a piece of silk that has been painted and appliquéd with single bluebell flowers.

Right inset: Dress up a plain white collar with subtly painted silk flowers appliquéd 'all in a row'.

1. Using a pencil, trace the larger bluebell shape sixteen times onto the Bondaweb backing paper (Fig 1). Space the shapes so that you can cut them out easily.

2. Roughly cut out each bluebell shape outside the pencil outline. Lay them onto the reverse side of the different coloured scraps of blue silk. Iron in place following the maker's instructions. Leave to cool. Cut out all the bluebell shapes, following the outlines.

3. Using the pair of compasses and the felt-tipped pen, draw out the pattern for the mirror onto the thin paper (Fig 2). Draw in the radiating lines to indicate the position for each flower. Iron the piece of white silk and tape it in place over the pattern, so that you can just see the lines through it.

4. Carefully peel off the backing paper from the back of the cut-out bluebells. Position them onto the silk, so that the radiating lines match up with the centre points on the flowers and the various colours are distributed evenly. When you are happy with the arrangement, iron them in place to the backing silk, as before.

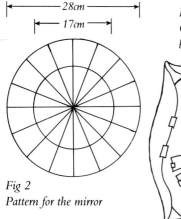

Fig 2
Pattern for the mirror

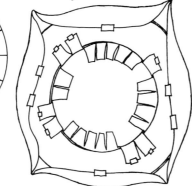

Fig 3
Glue the fabric tabs to the back of the card circle

5. Using an old saucer as a palette, mix up some of the two colours of fabric paints. Carefully paint the three veins and petal edges, as indicated by the shaded areas on the patterns, to give the flowers a three-dimensional look. (Iron the paint, as indicated, to fix permanently.)

6. Cut out a circle of thick card 28cm(11in) in diameter. Cut a circular hole in the centre 17cm(6¾in) in diameter. Cut out a piece of the wadding exactly the same size and glue it to the card circle. Lay the appliquéd silk face down on your work surface. Place the padded card circle on top, exactly in the centre of the design, with the wadding next to the silk. Trim the silk to a circle about 7.5cm(3in) larger than the card.

7. Using masking tape, temporarily tape the edges of the silk to the back of the card to hold it in position. Now cut out the central area of the silk to within 4cm(1½in) from the card frame. Snip into this excess fabric, all round to make small tabs. Fold the tabs back onto the card and glue in place (Fig 3). Work so that you are gluing pairs of tabs on opposite sides of the circle to keep the fabric smooth and taut. Leave the glue to dry.

8. Cut out two more 28cm(11in) diameter circles of the thick card. Cut out a circle from the centre of one of them to the exact size of the mirror. Glue the two circles together and then glue the mirror into the central cavity, to hold it securely (Fig 4).

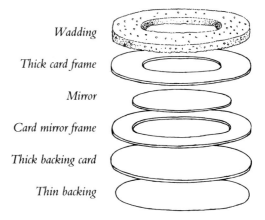

Wadding

Thick card frame

Mirror

Card mirror frame

Thick backing card

Thin backing

Fig 4
Assembly of card and mirror to make padded frame

Home-grown bluebells come in a surprising variety of tints from white, palest cobalt blues and mauves to deep ultramarine and even pink. Arrange them to maximum effect in a slim glass vase. There is no need to add any foliage, just push them loosely into the vase and the stems will gradually curve to make a lovely natural arrangement.

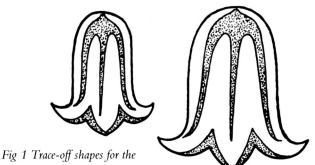

Fig 1 Trace-off shapes for the bluebell motifs

9. On the padded piece, remove the masking tape holding the outer edges of the fabric. Spread the card with glue and place the mirror piece on the back so that the mirror shows from the front of the padded frame. Pull the fabric edges to the back of the card and snip it into tabs. Glue the tabs to the card all round, working in opposite pairs, as before, to keep the fabric smooth and taut.

10. To make the hanging bow, fold the piece of blue silk in half lengthways, right side inside, and stitch down the long raw edges. Turn this tube of fabric right sides out and press. Tie a bow in the middle of the length of fabric and hand stitch the knot neatly at the back, so that it will not come undone. Trim both tails of the bow to the same length and glue the ends to the back of the frame, at the top, about 5cm(2in) apart.

11. To complete, cut out a 27cm(10½in) diameter circle of thin card and glue it to the frame back.

Transform a simple summer dress with these iron-on bluebell motifs on a detachable white collar.

The collar

Materials

- Ready-made white collar
- Scraps of lightweight silk in about five shades of blue
- Bondaweb fusible fleece
- Small sharp scissors
- Setacolour fabric paints in parma violet and white
- Fine watercolour brush

1. Iron the ready-made collar and lay it out flat on your ironing board. Then follow the initial instructions, paragraphs 1, 2, 4 and 5, for the mirror, positioning the small bluebell shapes evenly around the collar.

2. Attach the collar to the dress by hand with tiny running stitches. Remove from the dress before laundering and wash the collar carefully by hand.

White bouquet

lacy cushions and tablecloth

A bouquet composed simply of white flowers is, to me, real luxury.
Lace and frills continue the luxury look, so I have made a collection of
decorative white cushions and a tablecloth to enhance the theme.
The fresh blue-and-white voile curtains go beautifully with the
flowery stencilled walls and the checked bedspread adds
country charm to the scene.
To compensate for their lack of colour, white flowers are usually heavily
scented and beautifully formed, thus massing them together in one or
more arrangements makes a wonderful treat for the senses.
Mix larger flowers like delphiniums, stocks and stems of lilac with white
carnations and the delicate touch of gypsophila or even cow parsley
picked from the fields. Arrange them in classic blue-and-white china jugs
to set off the pale flowers beautifully.

Above: A simple bouquet of white garden roses massed together into a china dish is an easy and inexpensive way to achieve the look you want. Push the rose stems into an oasis block inside the dish to hold the flowers in the correct positions but aim for a casual rather than formal style to this arrangement.

Right: Pile them high and make them simply is my maxim with pretty bed cushions. Broderie anglaise, lace and ribbon all go together to make a fresh feminine look in a blue and white country cottage bedroom.

Square cushion

Materials

- Two 32cm(12¾in) squares of white broderie anglaise
- 30cm(12in) square cushion pad
- 3m(3yd) broderie-anglaise edging 6.5cm(2½in) wide
- 1m(1yd) narrow white spotted satin ribbon
- 1m(1yd) wider white checked satin ribbon

(NB Allow 1cm(⅜in) seams throughout)

1. Run a gathering thread along the raw edge of the broderie-anglaise edging and pull up the gathers to fit round the edge of one of the squares of broderie-anglaise fabric. Join the short ends with a french seam. Pin the frill in place all round, matching raw edges and with right sides together. Round off the corners slightly and stitch in place.

2. On the right side, stitch the checked ribbon in a square, about 4cm(1½in) away from the frill. Fold the ribbon once at the corners (Fig 1). Stitch the spotted ribbon onto the cover in the same way, about 1cm(⅜in) inside the first ribbon.

3. Place the other square of fabric on top of the cushion cover front piece. Have right sides together and raw edges matching. Pin and stitch round three sides making sure you do not catch the frill in the stitching. Turn right sides out and press. Insert the cushion pad and hand stitch the opening or add snap fasteners or tape ties to close.

The bolster

Materials

- Bolster cushion
- White sheeting to go round the cushion (with seam allowance) and about 40cm(16in) longer than the cushion, to allow for the frilled ends and pintucks
- Lace and ribbon lengths to go round the cushion:
  - 2 lengths double-frilled, broderie-anglaise edging, 10cm(4in) wide
  - 2 lengths picot-edged ribbon
  - 2 lengths broderie-anglaise edging, 3.5cm(1½in) wide
  - 2 lengths wide bias binding
  - 1 length straight-edged broderie anglaise, 10cm(4in) wide
  - 3 lengths 13mm(½in) wide satin ribbon

1. Fold over 10cm(4in) at each short end of the fabric and stitch to make a hem. Pin and stitch the narrow lacy edging and the picot-edged ribbon to the folded ends, on the right side.

2. Stitch the length of straight-edged lace down the centre of the cover. Make two pin tucks either side of this and then stitch the two lengths of the double-frilled edging outside this.

3. Lay the cover on the cushion, mark the position for the bias binding that will gather the ends in to hold the cushion in place.

4. Make a narrow pin tuck just inside the hem at each end. Stitch the bias-binding lengths to the reverse of the cover as marked. Fold the cover in half, right sides inside, and stitch along the raw edge. Turn right sides out and fit the cover onto the cushion. Make tiny holes near the seams and thread the ribbons through the bias-binding channels. Pull up the ribbons to gather the ends and tie in bows to complete.

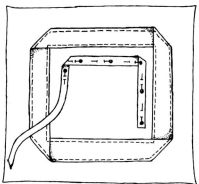

Fig 1
Fold the ribbon over once at the corners

Small round cushion

Materials

- Two 21cm(8in) circles of white broderie anglaise
- 1m(1yd) of broderie-anglaise edging, 9cm(3½in) wide
- 50cm(½yd) each of three different width and pattern satin ribbons
- Scraps of polyester wadding

1. Run a gathering thread along the edge of the broderie-anglaise edging and pull up the gathers to fit round the edge of one of the circles of fabric. Join the short ends with a french seam. Pin in place all round the circle, matching raw edges and with right sides together. Stitch in place.

2. Place the other circle of fabric on top of the cushion cover front piece. Have right sides together and raw edges matching. Pin and stitch round, leaving a gap for turning. Turn right sides out and press. Insert the wadding torn into small scraps and hand stitch the opening to neaten.

3. Lay the three pieces of ribbon together onto the work surface and tie them into a bow. Hand stitch this firmly to the front of the cushion, near the frill.

Tablecloth

Materials

- 60cm(24in) square of white broderie anglaise
- 3.20m(3½yd) of broderie-anglaise edging, 9cm(3½in) wide
- 2.40m(2¾yd) white spotted satin ribbon

1. Cut the broderie-anglaise edging into four equal pieces and pin them centrally onto the sides of the square of broderie anglaise. Have raw edges matching and right sides facing. Tack (baste) in place.

2. Fold the edging out flat and where the corners of the edging overlap, fold the pieces at right angles to mitre the corners neatly (Fig 2). Pin and stitch the mitres with right sides together and trim excess. Then stitch the edging to the cloth over the tacking (basting). Press flat.

3. Pin on the ribbon to cover the seam line, on the right side of the cloth. Fold at an angle at the corners so that the ribbon makes another mitre and lies flat. Tuck in the ends of the ribbon where they meet. Stitch all round, close to both sides of the ribbon.

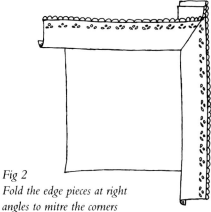

Fig 2
Fold the edge pieces at right angles to mitre the corners

You can quickly make this tiny lacy cloth to cover the top of a bedside table and match the bed cushions too.

Spring flowers
knotted rag rug

The wonderful combination of vibrant yellow and rich blue
always makes me think of spring bulbs. The daffodils and hyacinths,
narcissi and irises, yellow tulips and tiny grape hyacinths lighten our spring
days until they turn to 'glorious summer'. These fresh colours are one of
my favourite decorating themes, and this simple rag rug makes a lovely
feature in any room.

There are several different ways of making a rag rug, but I think this
hooking method makes one of the most attractive
and hard-wearing types. The tufts of fabric are knotted quite close
together in broad stripes to form a thick, soft mat. It takes quite a while to
complete but is a pleasant way to pass the time without a great deal of
concentration required. The only tool needed is an old-fashioned latch
hook, available from most craft shops.

Left: Making this charming country-style rag rug is an easy and absorbing pastime. It is fashioned from strips of cotton fabric, knotted onto a hessian backing. While away those long winter nights by the fireside, hooking this rug, ready for the first rays of spring sunshine.

Right: Rustic pots of grape hyacinths make a long-lasting spring decoration in a country kitchen.

Materials

- 126 x 85cm(50 x 33½in) piece of hessian
- Piece of canvas or sailcloth the same size, to back the rug
- Quantity of different cotton dress-and curtain-weight fabrics in blues and yellows, both plain and patterned (it will take about 3m/3yd of fabric to cover just the border area)
- Latch hook
- Carpet thread and a darning needle
- Black waterproof felt-tipped pen
- Long ruler
- Large 45-degree set square
- Piece of thick card 12cm(4¾in) wide

1. Using the felt-tipped pen and a ruler, mark the border all around the edge of the mat. Draw a line 5cm(2in) in from the raw edge to turn under and neaten at the end, then measure and draw a 12.5cm(5in) wide border inside this.

2. Using the set square and the felt-tipped pen, mark the central area into varying diagonal bands from about 4cm(1½in) to10 cm(4in) wide. Each of these bands will be worked in a different colour.

3. Start by cutting up some of the yellow fabrics for the border area. Cut the fabric into long 2cm(¾in) wide strips. Wind the strips round the piece of card and then cut top and bottom to make even-sized pieces (Fig 1).

Fig 1
Cut top and bottom to make even lengths

4. Push the latch hook through to the back of the hessian from the right side. Taking a small 'stitch' bring the hook out at the front again (Fig 2).

5. Fold a strip of fabric in half across the width and slip the fold into the hook (Fig 3). Pull the hook towards you through the hessian to make a loop.

6. Push the hook further through the loop and collect both free ends of the strip (Fig 4).

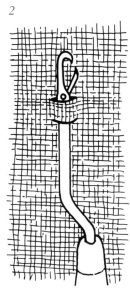

2

Fig 2
Push the latch hook through the hessian

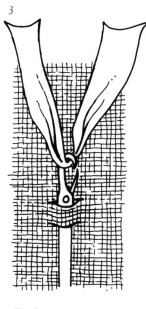

3

Fig 3
Slip the folded fabric into the hook

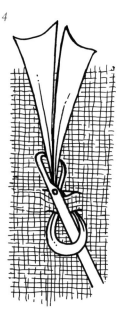

4

Fig 4
Push the hook through and collect both ends of the strip

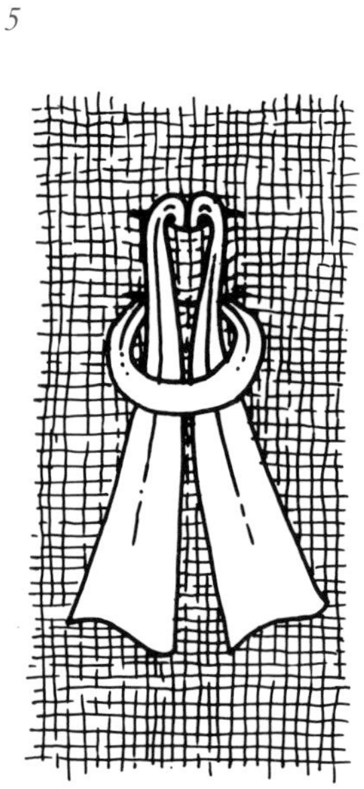

5

Fig 5
Pull the ends back through the loop and tighten

7. Pull these ends back through the loop, tighten and release (Fig 5). Stab the hook into the hessian about every 2cm(¾in) to make each tuft of the rug. Work the border area first, following the outline, then subsequent rows outside this until you reach the turning for the hem. Always try to keep the knots facing the same way for an even texture.

8. Work the diagonal bands in definite stripes of colour. Work in straight lines following the drawn pattern, mixing the fabrics so that you have some distinct stripes of colour and some blending subtly from light to dark.

9. When you have completed the rug, you may need to stretch it gently to shape by hand, either alone or with the help of another person. When you have done this, turn the edges under 5cm(2in) to neaten. Slip stitch, with carpet thread, all round. Trim the surface of the rug slightly with sharp scissors to give it an even pile.

10. Turn under the edges of the sailcloth or canvas and hand stitch to the back of the mat using back stitch (Fig 6). This helps the rug to keep its shape and makes it more hardwearing. To clean the rug, hang it up out of doors and beat it to remove dust and dirt, in the old-fashioned way.

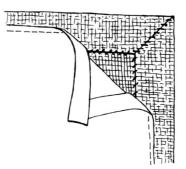

Fig 6
Turn under the edges
of the sailcloth

Detail showing the many strips of patterned cotton fabric that go into making this rag rug. Notice the subtle blending of fabrics from one colour to the next.

31

Violet
embroidered tray cloth, napkins and sachets

Shy little violets always make me think of Victorian ladies, tea-time and lace, so I have combined all these images into a collection of embroidered cloths and sachets. The lacy edging with the woven ribbon trimming and bows completes the Victorian look.

Above: Violets are so small they need to be seen by themselves, in a tiny container like this pretty little china basket. Display on a small dressing table or tea tray where it can be seen close up.

Right: Violets embroidered in satin stitch and long-and-short stitch are strewn around the edge of a lacy tray cloth. Embroider a single flower in the corner of a matching napkin.

Inset: Two violets entwined on a romantic, heart-shaped sachet to decorate the dressing table.

Materials for the embroideries

- DMC Zweigart Edinburgh linen 3217 in white
- DMC stranded cotton (floss) in the following colours: 550, 209, 552, 211, 307, 3364, 3345 and 3363.
- Cotton lace for trimming: 2.5cm(1in) wide for cloth and mats; 4cm(1½in) wide for heart-shaped sachets; and 13mm(½in) wide for jam-pot covers
- Narrow satin ribbon; pale green for cloth and mats, mauve for sachets
- Scraps of polyester wadding
- Tracing paper
- Fine black waterproof felt-tipped pen
- Soluble embroidery marker pen
- Crewel embroidery needles
- Embroidery frame (optional)

To make the tray cloth, napkins and mats

1. Trace all the violet patterns onto tracing paper, using the black waterproof pen (Figs 1 and 2).

Fig 1
Full-size patterns for the violet motifs

2. Cut out a piece of linen for the tray cloth. Place this over the traced pattern so that the main motif of the design will be near one corner. Pin the pattern in place all round the edge. Using the soluble marker pen, draw in the lines of the pattern onto the linen. Move the tracing paper and place it so that the line of single violets follows the edge of the fabric. Then trace, as before. Continue in this way to complete the design, turning as you reach the corners so that the line of violets follows on evenly.

3. Use three strands of stranded cotton (floss) for the stitching. Cut it into pieces about 50cm(20in) long to avoid tangling as you sew. You can work in an embroidery frame if you wish.

4. Following the stitch diagrams, begin by stitching the violet petals in long-and-short stitch. Shade the colours on each petal using the photographs as a guide. Stitch the yellow centres in satin stitch.

5. Next embroider the leaves, also in long-and-short stitch. Stitch each half of the leaf as a separate shape, and then add the veins in stem stitch in a darker green. Sew the veins down the centre of each leaf, with smaller veins branching off either side, as shown on the photograph.

6. Now embroider the stems in a paler green using stem stitch. Make two tiny chain stitches either side of the stems, where indicated. (Follow these instructions for embroidering the violets when making all the different items.)

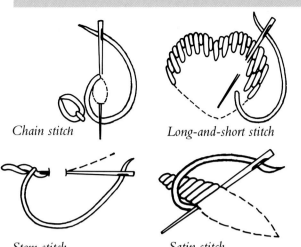

Chain stitch

Long-and-short stitch

Stem stitch

Satin stitch

Close-up showing the detail of the main embroidery motif on the corner of the tray cloth.

7. Press the back of the stitching before making it up. Lay the embroidered fabric face down onto a piece of clean cotton cloth. Lay another piece on top and press with a steam iron, to raise the texture of the stitches, rather than flattening them.

8. Zigzag stitch all round the edge of the linen. Then stitch cotton lace all round, on the right side, pleating it at the corners. Insert pale green ribbon into the holes in the lace. Make tiny matching napkins and mats in the same way using a single flower motif.

To make the heart-shaped sachet

Embroider the two entwined violets onto a piece of linen and stitch along the inner heart shape in mauve stem stitch. Cut out along the outer heart shape. Cut another piece of linen the same size. Place them right sides together, and stitch all round, leaving a small gap for turning. Turn right sides out and stuff lightly with scraps of wadding. Push in the raw edges and hand stitch to neaten. Run a

The voilet motifs embroidered on a tiny sachet and a lace-edged cover for a bowl of pot-pourri.

gathering thread close to the lower edge of about 1m(1yd) of the wide cotton lace.Pull up the gathers to fit round the sachet and pin in place. Hand stitch the lace on neatly and make a small ribbon loop and bow to complete.

To make the square sachet

Embroider a single violet onto a small piece of linen. Cut another piece the same size and pin this behind it, right sides outside. Draw a line to frame the violet and embroider this in stem stitch through both thicknesses of fabric. When you have almost completed this line, insert some wadding and pot pourri and finish the stitching. Now trim the sachet just outside the stitching using pinking shears.

To make the jam-pot or pot-pourri covers

Embroider the motif of two entwined violets onto the centre of a 20cm(8in) diameter circle of linen. Zigzag stitch all round and sew on the narrow lace to decorate the edge. Place over a jam pot or dish of pot pourri and hold with an elastic band. Tie round with narrow satin ribbonto complete.

Fig 2 Trace off shapes for border pattern

Daffodil

Victorian-style needlepoint picture

What could be more inspiring than Wordsworth's
'host of golden daffodils'? These lovely flowers seem to bring out the
artist in just about everyone. Daffodils are one of the least expensive
flowers to buy or grow, and yet they bring one of the greatest rewards
with their fresh colour, scent and the promise of sunshine.
There are so many different types of daffodil now, yet the simple plain
yellow flower has a charm all its own.
I started this design by drawing just a few flowers in different positions,
and developed the drawings into this needlepoint picture.
The naturalistic style is combined with a formal border pattern
inspired by Victorian tile designs.

*Above: Mix daffodils and narcissi with sprigs of cow
parsley and herbs from the garden to make a sweet
smelling decoration.*

*Opposite:The completed needlepoint makes a lovely
picture, or it could be stitched into an elegant cushion cover
that would look perfect in a conservatory.*

Materials

- 40 cm(16in) square picture frame (inside
  measurement) with backing board
- 60cm(24in) square of double-thread white
  tapestry canvas, 10 threads per inch(25mm)
- Tapestry frame or carpet tape
- Appletons tapestry wools (yarns)
  (each skein is 12 strands) as follows:
  4 skeins of 561
  3 skeins each of 551 and 991
  2 skeins each of 553, 997, 311, 352, 293, 876,
  153, 966 and 462
  1 skein each of 844, 554, 474, 475, 763, 851,
  253, 294, 853 and 322
- Size 24 tapestry needles
- Pins
- Darning needle
- Strong linen thread

1. Start by binding the edge of the canvas with
tape, or mounting it onto a frame. Then choose
which stitch you prefer (see Stitches) and follow the
instructions below to stitch the daffodil picture
from the chart and colour key (Fig 1) overleaf.

Generally, it is best to start stitching in the centre of
the design and work out towards the edge,
finishing with the background. This is the best way
to use a charted design, to avoid making mistakes in
counting the squares. You should always mark the
centre of the canvas, both vertically and
horizontally with a line of tacking (basting), to

match the centre lines on the charts. Count and mark the outer edge as well. Do not be tempted to mark the canvas with a pencil line as this will rub off onto the wool and discolour it. Remember that each square on the chart represents one stitch on the needlepoint.

2. Cut your wool (yarn) into manageable lengths. About 75cm(30in) is ideal as you don't have to re-thread the needle too often, and the wool (yarn) does not fray from continually being pulled through the canvas.

3. Begin stitching by bringing the wool (yarn) up from the underside of the canvas. Leave about 5cm(2in) of wool (yarn) at the back and hold this in place while you make the first few stitches over it, to stop the stitching coming undone. Work the stitches, following the diagrams and chart, then finish off the thread by weaving it behind two or three stitches. Then cut off the end, to leave about 5cm(2in) of wool (yarn) which can be incorporated in the back of the work as you go. You can move to another area of the same colour without fastening off the wool (yarn) but the next area should be a maximum distance of 2cm(¾in) away. If you try to carry the wool (yarn) any further, there will be too many strands criss-crossing the back of the needlepoint and the finished work will suffer.

Try to keep the stitch tension regular. You should aim for a smooth even look, where the wool (yarn) is not so tight that the canvas shows through, nor so loose that loops form on the front of the needlepoint.

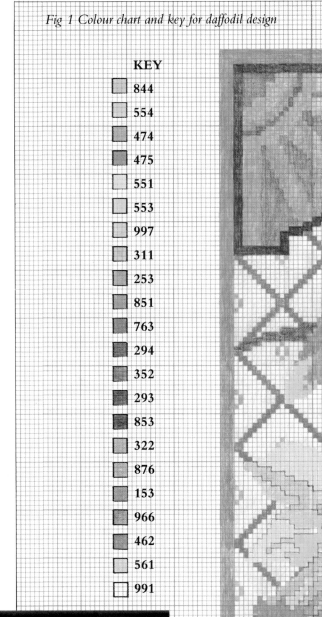

Fig 1 Colour chart and key for daffodil design

KEY

	844
	554
	474
	475
	551
	553
	997
	311
	253
	851
	763
	294
	352
	293
	853
	322
	876
	153
	966
	462
	561
	991

Close-up of the needlepoint showing the subtle colours that form the border pattern.

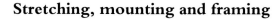
Stitches

The stitches used are half cross stitch, tent stitch or basket-weave tent stitch. They all look the same on the front of the canvas and are quick and easy to work.

Half cross stitch is the most economical with the amount of wool (yarn) needed, but its one slight drawback is that it tends to pull the canvas diagonally out of shape. This means that unless you work in a frame, the finished needlepoint needs to be dampened and stretched back into shape. This is not too much of a problem, and it has the two-fold advantage of smoothing out any slight irregularities in the tension of the stitching at the same time.

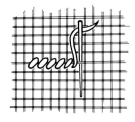

Tent stitch is also easy to do, but because it makes a longer diagonal on the back of the work, it uses more wool (yarn), as well as distorting the canvas.

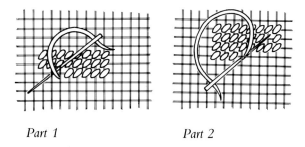

Part 1   *Part 2*

Basket-weave tent stitch causes the least distortion and is ideal for the larger background areas. You can use a combination of these stitches to suit the size of the area to be worked.

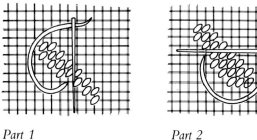

Part 1   *Part 2*

Stretching, mounting and framing

It is recommended that needlepoint is stretched and framed professionally for the best results, but if you want to do it yourself, here are the instructions.

For stretching you will need a large piece of blockboard, a set square and ruler, a plant spray, several sheets of clean white blotting paper and good quality drawing pins or a staple-gun.

1. Start by spraying the back of your needlepoint with water so that it is very damp but not soaking wet. Lay the sheets of blotting paper out on the blockboard and spray them lightly with water. Place the needlepoint face down on the blotting paper and pull it into shape with your hands. You may have to pull quite strongly and then check the accuracy with the set square and ruler.

2. Pin or staple along one edge, through the canvas only, stretching it as you go. Now pin the opposite edge, pulling it really taut. Pin the other two sides in the same way, starting at the centre point on each side and working out towards the corners.

This unusual wreath of daffodils and narcissi is made by cutting the stems quite short and pushing them into a ring of oasis. You will need to keep the oasis really moist, perhaps standing it in a container of water at night to keep the flowers alive for the maximum amount of time.

3. Lightly spray the whole surface of the needlepoint and then leave it in a warm place to dry gently over one or two days. Do not be tempted to dry it too fast against a radiator or you may damage the work.

4. When it is quite dry and flat, remove the pins or staples. Sometimes you may need to repeat this process if your work is very badly distorted.

5. To make the picture, you will need to mount the canvas onto a piece of thick board that has been cut slightly undersize to fit loosely into the frame. This will allow for the extra canvas folded around the edge. The stitching can stop about 5mm(¼in) from the edge, as this will be hidden under the frame rebate.

6. Position the design centrally on the board, and then turn the board and canvas over carefully so that the needlepoint is face down. Insert pins into the edge of the board to hold the needlepoint in place. Using a darning needle and strong linen thread, lace the canvas round the board (Fig 2).

Work across the centre vertically and horizontally then diagonally, pulling the canvas evenly. Lift and check the front of the work occasionally to make sure the design has not been pulled out of place. Remove the pins as you go.

Fig 2 Lacing the needlepoint onto the board for mounting

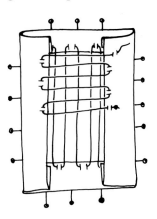

7. When the needlepoint is firmly and evenly mounted, place it into the frame, and secure.

Tulip
dining accessories

I was lucky enough to find this lovely chintz fabric ('Tulipa' by Osborne and Little) featuring my favourite striped tulips, and also a very useful border pattern which suggested these kitchen and dining accessories.

The fabric is padded and then machine quilted through the layers, carefully following the outlines to accentuate the flowers. The thick padding acts as insulation on the tea cosy and bread basket, and as protection from the heat on the oven glove and table mats.

Tulips look especially good when they are arranged simply in quantities of one colour and type. As they stand in water they naturally bend into beautiful curves that change subtly as the days go by. These delicately coloured blooms streaked with green develop from tightly folded buds to flamboyant open shapes with the petals folded right back to the stems.

Materials

- Tulipa fabric (about 2m(2yd) will make all the accessories)
- 113g(4oz) polyester wadding
- Bias binding in toning colour, 2.5cm(1in) wide
- 3m(3yd) narrow satin ribbon
- Thick card or 2mm(⅛in) thick perspex
- Matching sewing cottons
- Small round basket
- 35cm(14in) elastic,1.5cm(⅝in) wide
- Squared graph paper

Right: Remove all but the topmost pair of leaves on each tulip stem, as you arrange them. Use a large container and top it up with water frequently as the tulips drink copious amounts!

Left: An unusual padded tea cosy that allows you to pour the tea and top up the pot with hot water, without removing the cover.

Basic quilting

Unless otherwise stated, the quilted areas for each article should be stitched first and then the pieces can be made up into the finished items. To do this, cut out the top fabric, wadding and backing to the required shape, which is given slightly oversize to allow for shrinkage after quilting.

Next, tack (baste) the layers together carefully before you begin quilting. This is a very important stage in the process, as the layers can easily slip out of place while you are stitching. The wadding should be laid between the layers of fabric and the right sides of the fabric should be on the outside. Use a fine needle and thread, so as not to mark the fabric unnecessarily, and start tacking (basting) with a knot on the right side. Start stitching in the centre of the fabric and work outwards to each corner. Then tack (baste) vertically and horizontally in lines about 10cm(4in) apart. Lastly, tack (baste) all round, near the raw edges. Work with medium-length stitches and do not pull the thread too tightly.

Using a medium-length, straight machine-stitch, follow the outline of the flowers on the patterned fabric to accentuate them. Pull the threads through to the back of the work and tie off securely.

A collection of matching table accessories with thickly padded table mats, a covered basket for warm rolls and even simple covers for the jam pots.

To make the table mats

1. Cut out two pieces of the fabric and one piece of wadding to measure 36 x 26.5cm(14 x 10½in) for each table mat. Choose the position of the design carefully for the front of the mat and use up odd pieces for the back. Tack (baste) the layers together as described.

2. Machine-stitch round the flowers, leaves and stems so that they stand out from the background.

3. Using a cup and a pencil, draw rounded corners onto the quilted fabric. Zigzag stitch all round, following the raw edge and the pencilled curves, to neaten. Then trim off the excess fabric at the corners, close to the zigzag stitching.

4. Open out one side of the bias binding and pin it round the edge of the mat, with raw edges matching and right sides together (Fig 1). Stitch all round the mat following the fold line on the binding. Overlap and turn under the short ends to neaten. Fold the binding over the raw edge and slip stitch the folded edge to the back of the mat neatly. Remove the tacking (basting) stitches to complete. Make up the other mats in the same way.

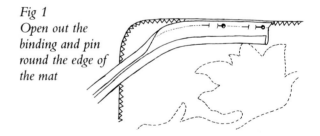

Fig 1
Open out the binding and pin round the edge of the mat

To make the basket

1. Measure the top of the basket and make a padded lid that will rest on the top edge, using the same method as for the table mats. Hand stitch two long pieces of satin ribbon on opposite sides of the lid to tie onto the basket handles.

2. Using the inside measurement, make a padded mat for the base of the basket in the the same way.

To make the jam-pot covers

Using pinking shears, simply cut out circles of fabric about 10cm(4in) larger than the top of the pot. Try to place one of the smaller flowers in the centre of the circle. Place over the pot and hold with an elastic band. Tie round with a length of narrow satin ribbon to decorate.

To make the oven glove

1. For the main shape, cut out two pieces of the flowered fabric and two pieces of wadding to measure 19 x 69cm(7½ x 27in). Tack (baste) the layers together using the double thickness of wadding and then quilt as described.

2. For the end pieces, cut four pieces of flowered fabric and two pieces of wadding 19cm(7½in) square. Tack (baste) and quilt these in pairs in the same way. Turn in the raw edges of fabric on one side of each piece and hand stitch to neaten.

3. Pin the quilted end pieces at either end of the main piece, with right sides uppermost and raw edges matching. Tack (baste) in place. Round off the corners as for the table mats and bind the edges of the oven glove in the same way. Remove the tacking (basting) and stitch a loop of folded binding to the centre of one side for hanging.

Plain green bias binding sets off the floral fabric and neatens the edges of this rather luxurious oven glove.

To make the tea cosy

1. Draw out the pattern for the side of the tea cosy onto squared graph paper (each square represents one inch(25mm) (Fig 2).

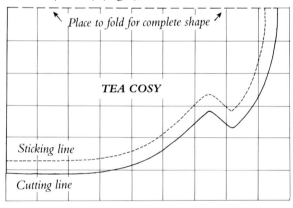

Fig 2 Pattern for the tea cosy (each square represents 1in(25mm))

2. Using the pattern, cut out four pieces in fabric and two pieces in wadding. Tack (baste) one piece of the wadding to the back of one piece of fabric. Quilt round the flower motif as described. Place another piece of the fabric over this, with right sides together and pin in place. Stitch round, 1cm(⅜in) away from the raw edge, leaving the straight lower edge open. Trim the wadding away from the seamline, then turn right sides out and press. Make up the other half of the tea cosy in the same way.

3. Cut out a 14.5cm(5¾in) diameter circle of thick card or perspex. Cut out two circles of fabric about 2cm(¾in) larger and sandwich the stiffening between them, with right sides outside. Tack (baste) all round, close to the stiffening.

*Fig 3
Stitch the side pieces to the circular base*

4. With right sides together, hand stitch the lower edge of each quilted side piece to the edge of the stiffened circle (Fig 3). Trim this seam with pinking shears near the stitching. Hand stitch the side pieces together for about 2.5cm(1in) near the base and turn right sides out.

5. Cut a piece of fabric 6 x 80cm(2⅜ x 31½in). Fold it in half lengthways with the right side inside. Stitch 1cm(⅜in) from the long edge to make a tube. Turn right side out and press. Insert a 35cm(14in) piece of elastic and stitch the ends together firmly. Turn in the ends of the fabric and stitch to neaten. Place the teapot inside the cosy and use the gathered fabric band to fasten it at the top.

Peony
needlepoint chair seat

These huge, vibrantly coloured flowers are at their best in early summer when they bloom profusely in many gardens. Although they are quite complex looking flowers, their richness of colour makes them an ideal subject for a needlepoint design, with their unusual leaves forming an outer border to the composition.

Peonies come in a variety of wonderful colours, ranging from deep cerise and wine red through to the palest rose-pink and delicate white. The flowers are sometimes single but mostly double, with the petals packed tightly into the centre of each rose-shaped bloom.

Materials

- Double-thread, natural coloured tapestry canvas, 10 holes per inch(25mm), 10cm(4in) larger all round than your chair seat
- Tapestry frame or carpet tape
- DMC tapisserie wools (yarns):
  6 skeins minimum of 7429 (depending on size of chair seat as this is background colour)
  2 skeins each of 7138, 7136, 7132, 7406, 7373, 7376 and 7427
  1 skein each of 7205, 7204, 7173, 7746, 7404, 7428, 7375, 7600, 7602, 7804, 7219 and 7135
- Size 24 tapestry needle
- Drawing pins
- Round-headed pins
- Tack hammer

Above: Peonies look marvellous mixed with a few other flowers of similar colour such as sweet williams, carnations or stocks. Follow the same colour scheme when you choose the flower containers and surround the group with pink accessories for maximum impact.

When arranging the peonies strip off most of the foliage from the stems first so that they don't make the water slimy.

Opposite: The peony needlepoint design is centered on a background of dark forest green and will fit comfortably onto the seat area of most chairs. Stitch the background to the shape you require, to fit your chair seat. This intricately carved Victorian nursing chair seems the ideal place to display this flamboyantly coloured piece of needlework but it would look just as striking stitched into cushions or decorating a firescreen.

To make the chair seat

Before working out the shape for your chair cover, it is advisable to have an old chair re-upholstered, or at least to remove the original cover and recover the seat with calico. Keep the old cover, as it is very useful as a pattern for your needlepoint. If you do not have an old cover, measure the seat accurately and draw out a pattern to the correct size and shape, taking into account the way the chair back and legs fit onto the seat. Draw this shape onto the canvas, adding at least 7.5cm(3in) all round. Cut the canvas well outside this pattern line if you are going to mount it in a frame for working the needlepoint.

Start by binding the edge of the canvas with tape, or mounting it onto a frame. Then follow the instructions given for stitching the daffodil needlepoint picture (page 36), using the chart and colour key opposite. Position the peonies centrally in the pattern area, slightly nearer the front than the back of the chair to make it look central.

When you have completed the needlepoint, cover your chair seat in the following way.

Lay the needlepoint over the chair seat and pin it in place at the centre point. Pull the canvas taut and pin temporarily with drawing pins, a little way from the edge of the chair seat. Work so that you are pinning first at the top and bottom, then at opposite sides, and then pin between these points, pulling the canvas taut. Make any pleats at the corners as small and flat as possible, for a smooth finish. Trim away any excess canvas from these areas. Now cut off all the surplus canvas from the edges and turn under the raw edge to make a neat hem. Hammer in the round-headed pins all round the edge of the seat. The pins should be very close together so that you cannot see the edge of the canvas. (It is sometimes helpful to draw in a line for the pins to ensure they are placed in a straight line.)

Colour chart and key for the peony design.

KEY

■	7138
■	7136
■	7205
■	7204
■	7132
■	7173
■	7746
■	7375
■	7600
■	7804
■	7602
■	7219
■	7136
■	7135
■	7429
■	7404
■	7406
■	7428
■	7373
■	7376
■	7427

Pansy

stencilled sachets, cushion and fabric

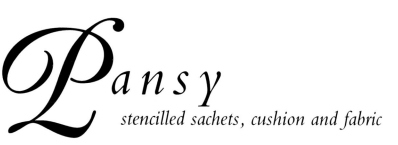

Simple pansies, in all their shapes, sizes and
colours, are delightful flowers that bloom
profusely almost all the year round. Each pansy
flower looks rather like a face, and the petal
shapes can be easily transposed into a most
effective stencil motif. Here, three different
flowers have been printed onto fine, white
cotton fabric to make a tiny cushion, scented
sachets and even a length of fabric that could
be used as a tablecloth or curtain.

You can make a lovely display of pansies
indoors, early in the season, pushing whole
plants into pretty patterned tureens and basins
to hide the soil. This is an attractive and
economical way to use pansies, as the flowers
last so much longer while they are still growing
on the plant. Later, you can move the plants to
outdoor tubs or flower beds to flower
again and again.

*Scatter stencilled pansies all over a length of white cotton
lawn. Then make up the fabric into charming little curtains to
dress a tiny cottage window.*

Pansy stencil

Materials

- Stencil card or clear acetate sheet
- Fine black waterproof felt-tipped pen
- Sharp craft knife
- Cutting mat
- Small stencil brushes
- Stencil crayons in yellow, blue and mauve
- White cotton chintz fabric
- Scrap of pale-blue cotton chintz fabric
- Low-tack tape
- Polyester wadding

Display a group of the pansy sachets on long loops of ribbon hung from the top edge of simple white curtains or bed drapes to subtly scent your room.

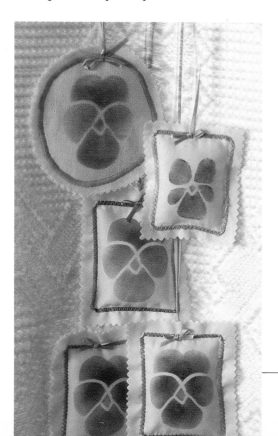

1. Following the shapes on this page, trace off the three sizes of pansy flowers. Transfer these onto the stencil card or acetate, using the felt-tipped pen, leaving about 5cm(2in) space all round each motif. Cut out the petal shapes carefully, using the craft knife and a cutting mat (Fig 1). Trim round each flower so that you have three separate stencils.

2. Prepare the fabric by washing and ironing, and then tape it flat to your work surface. Rub the tip of each crayon onto kitchen paper to remove the protective coating and then rub the crayon onto the edge of the stencil sheet and collect the colour on a stencil brush. Beginning with the yellow in the centre of the flower, dab the colour on carefully so that it does not spread into the other petals. Using a clean brush and a circular motion, gently stencil some blue round the outer edge of the flower. Collect some mauve onto another brush and stencil up to the centre of the pansy, blending the colours for a natural effect. Experiment with different colour combinations to vary the design.

Fig 1 Cutting out the stencil

Fig 2 Blending the stencil colours

For the sachets, stencil each flower separately leaving about 3cm(1¼in) all round as a border. For the cushion, stencil one large flower in the centre of a 22cm(9in) square of chintz, one medium-sized flower near each corner and a small flower in between.

To make the patterned material, simply stencil all three sizes of flower randomly over the fabric, making sure they are all the same way up and evenly spaced. Leave the stencilling to dry for a few hours then press with a hot iron, under a clean cloth, to fix the dyes.

To make the sachets

1. Cut out each stencilled flower to a rectangle or a circle and cut another piece of fabric the same size for the back of the sachet. Place the two pieces together, with right sides outside, and stitch round three sides, about 1.5cm(½in) from the edge.

2. Fill the bag with a spoonful of pot-pourri or lavender and stitch up the last side to close.

3. Zigzag stitch a line of narrow satin ribbon over the first row of stitches and trim the edges of the white fabric neatly with pinking shears. Finish with a long loop of the same ribbon and a tiny bow.

To make the tiny cushion

1. Using pinking shears, cut a 4.5 x 170cm(1¾ x 68in) strip of white chintz and a 3.5 x 170cm(1⅜ x 68in) strip of pale-blue chintz. Place the blue piece on top of the white piece, with one long edge matching, and run a gathering thread 1cm(⅜in) from this edge. Pull up the gathers to form a frill.

2. Place the frill round the edge of the stencilled square, with the right sides facing and with the raw edges matching. Spread out the gathers evenly to fit, curving the frill round at the corners. Pin and stitch all round (Fig 3).

3. Cut out another square of white chintz for the back of the cushion and stitch it in place, round three sides, over the frill. Turn the cushion the right side out and fill with polyester wadding. Pin and hand stitch the opening to neaten.

Fig 3 Stitching the frill round the edge of the cushion

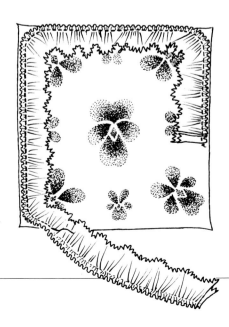

Print a symmetrical design of pansies onto plain white chintz, trim with a double frill in blue and white and turn it into a tiny decorative pillow to display on a bed or sofa.

Ranunculus

cushions and tea cosy

These wonderful, vibrantly coloured flowers immediately suggest the vivid hues of Indian shot silk. The cushions and tea cosy are made using a modern version of Italian quilting, stitched in straight lines and embellished with rows of satin ribbon. This is much quicker and easier to do than the traditional method and it is perfect used in a modern setting.

Materials

- Silk dupion in vivid shades of cerise, red and orange: about 50cm(½ yd) for each cushion
- Similar amount of stiff cotton backing fabric
- White polycotton and polyester wadding for lining the tea cosy
- Satin ribbon in varying colours and widths from 3mm to 15mm(⅛ in to ⅝ in)
- Silk threads to match
- Quilting wool (yarn)
- Large darning needle or bodkin
- Medium piping cord
- Cushion pads
- Ruler
- Tailor's chalk pencil

Left: Choose an unusual container like this flamboyant teapot to display a multicoloured bunch of ranunculus. Simply cut the stems to about the same length and strip off the foliage. Arrange the blooms casually in the top of the teapot and display the decorative lid alongside.

Right: Show off the cushions in a vivid colour scheme. The parallel lines of the Italian quilting are beautifully echoed by the hand-painted stripes on this bedroom wall and the formality of the stripes contrasts well with the flowery pottery.

Basic quilting

1. Cut out the required amount of silk dupion for each project, adding about 2.5cm(1in) extra all round, to allow for slight shrinkage as you quilt. Cut a piece of backing fabric the same size and tack (baste) the two layers together with right sides outside. Make several rows of tacking (basting), both vertically and horizontally, and one row around the edge.

2. Using a ruler and a tailor's chalk pencil, mark a diagonal line centrally across the silk, for your first line of stitching. Thread up your machine in a toning silk thread and stitch along the marked line in straight stitch. Using the presser foot as a guide, stitch another line parallel to this, across the fabric. You can also use an adjustable quilting gauge to help keep the lines really accurate (Fig 1). Continue in this way, leaving smaller and larger gaps between the lines until you have covered the piece of fabric completely. The spaces between the lines should range from about 7mm(¼in) to 3cm(1¼in).

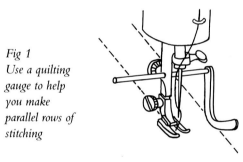

*Fig 1
Use a quilting gauge to help you make parallel rows of stitching*

3. Lay some pieces of satin ribbon along the quilting in the larger gaps between the rows of stitching. Pin the ribbons in place to make an attractive arrangement of colours and widths. Stitch the ribbon in position using rows of straight stitch, close to the edges. To attach very narrow ribbon you can use zigzag stitch in a contrasting colour for a more textured effect.

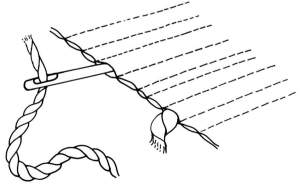

Fig 2 Thread the channels with quilting wool, using a bodkin

The rich silk and ribbon quilting makes the perfect tea cosy to accompany this rose-strewn teapot and striped tea-set.

4. Remove the tacking stitches from the fabric and press on the wrong side. Thread a large darning needle or bodkin with a long length of quilting wool (yarn). Pull the ends of the wool (yarn) equally through the needle then thread this through the narrower channels of your quilting to pad them (Fig 2). Cut the ends of wool (yarn) level with the raw edge of the fabric. Continue this over the whole piece of fabric, padding some of the wider channels with several strands of wool. Leave some channels unpadded to maximize the effect.

5. Stitch all round the edge of the fabric to hold the wool in place then measure and trim the quilting to the correct size leaving a 1.5cm(⅝in) seam allowance.

To make the cushions

1. Make up one quilted cushion front as described. Cut the fabric to the same size as your cushion pad with the extra amount for seams all round.

2. Cover your piping cord with 4cm(1½in) wide bias strips of silk, joining pieces where necessary. Fold this round the cord and pin and stitch close to the cord, using a zipper foot . Pin the covered cord round the edge of the cushion front, on the right side and with raw edges matching. When you reach the corners, snip into the raw edge of the seam allowance on the cord and bend it round to make a curve (Fig 3). Where the ends of the cord meet, pull back the covering fabric and trim the cord exactly to length. Join the raw ends of fabric, with right sides together and then machine-stitch the piping all round the cushion, close to the cord.

3. Cut out a matching piece of silk for the cushion back. Place this over the cushion front, with right sides facing and raw edges matching. Pin in place

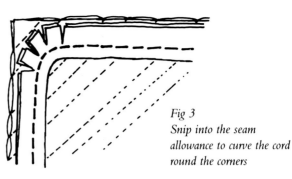

Fig 3
Snip into the seam allowance to curve the cord round the corners

and stitch round three sides following the previous line of stitching. Trim the excess fabric from the corners and turn the cover right sides out. Insert the cushion pad and hand stitch the opening to neaten. Alternatively, you could insert a zip here, to make it easier to take the cover off for cleaning.

4. Make round cushions in the same way, adding a collar round the edge if your cushion pad is particularly thick.

To make the tea cosy

1. Cut out two pieces of silk and backing fabric to measure 28 x 36cm(11 x 14in). Quilt the two pieces as described to make the back and the front of the tea cosy. Round off the top two corners on both pieces. Draw round a small plate or saucer to make smooth, accurate curves and then cut along the lines.

2. Make up some covered piping cord, as for the cushions, and pin this round three sides of one of the quilted pieces, leaving the lower, straight edge unpiped (Fig 4). Place the cord on the right side of the fabric, with raw edges matching, and stitch close to the cord. Pin the other quilted piece over the top, with right sides facing, and stitch through all the layers along the previous line of stitching.

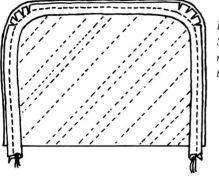

Fig 4
Stitch the piping round three sides of the tea cosy

3. Using sharp scissors, cut notches into the curved areas of the seam allowance and then turn the tea cosy right sides out. Turn under a tiny hem, along the raw edge, and hand stitch to neaten.

4. For the padded part of the tea cosy, cut out four pieces of white polycotton and two pieces of wadding to measure 33 x 25cm(13 x 10in). Stitch the pieces of fabric together, in pairs, along one long edge. Turn right sides out and sandwich one piece of wadding between each pair of fabric pieces. Pin the fabric round the wadding and, using a saucer as before, draw two lines to curve the top two corners. Cut to shape and then stitch through all the layers to join both padded pieces. Trim the seam close to the stitching.

5. Slip the quilted cover over the padded cosy and fold the lower edge to the inside. Slip stitch this in place to the padding. The top cover can then be easily removed for washing.

Sweet pea
covered baskets

Sweet peas have the most marvellous scent and are available in a whole array of pale ice-cream colours and rich dark reds and purples. These colours were the inspiration for my collection of fabric-covered baskets. This craft is an easy way to make lovely gifts using scraps of fabric and inexpensive baskets.

Although sweet peas are usually grown as a flower to use in arrangements, they can be trained to flower on a well-supported trellis making a lovely light screen to separate different areas of your garden. They last well as cut flowers and have a delicate butterfly shape which is pretty with lightweight foliage.

Above: A mixed bunch of sweet peas, straight from the garden, simply arranged in a plain green vase makes a display to scent a whole room. Their colours can be pale and pretty or deep and exotic.

Opposite: Small baskets make delightful gifts when covered and decorated with pretty patterned fabric. They can be used for storing jewellery, baby toiletries, sewing accessories, make-up or even bread rolls.

Provençal-print basket

Materials

- Small wicker basket, about 23cm(9in) high
- 40cm(½yd) Provençal-printed cotton fabric
- 20cm(¼yd) toning shot silk
- Matching cottons

1. Cut a very long, 4cm(1½in) wide, strip of printed cotton. Press a tiny hem all down one long side, and use the strip to bind the handle of the basket, with the hemmed edge overlapping the raw edge (Fig 1). Stitch both ends inside the basket neatly.

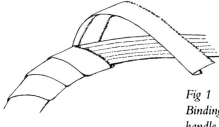

*Fig 1
Binding the basket handle with folded fabric*

2. Measure from the top edge of the basket, down the side to the centre of the base. Cut a piece of the printed fabric to this width and make the length about 2cm(¾in) longer than the circumference of the basket. This is the main piece.

3. Place the short raw edges together, with right sides inside and stitch, taking a 1cm(³/₈in) seam. Turn right sides out and press. Run a gathering thread close to the lower edge.

4. Cut a strip of the printed fabric 8cm(3in) wide and twice the circumference of the basket. Fold in half lengthways, with the right sides outside, and run a gathering thread close to the raw edges. Pull up the gathers to make a frill to fit along the top edge of the main piece. Tack (baste) it to the right side, with raw edges matching. Neaten the ends of the frill by hand, where they meet.

5. Make a lining out of the silk to the same size as the main piece. Stitch the side seam and run a gathering thread along the lower edge in the same way. Pull up the gathers and tie off tightly to close the end of the lining. Cut a 5cm(3in) diameter circle of silk and run a gathering thread all round the edge. Pull up the gathers slightly to draw the raw edges over to the wrong side and press. Slip stitch this circle to the base of the lining, on the right side, to cover the raw edges neatly.

6. Place the lining inside the basket and slip the printed cover over the outside. Turn over the raw edge of the lining and slip stitch it to the frill to cover the stitching line. Pull up the gathers on the lower edge of the printed fabric so that the cover fits the basket. Make a circle of cotton fabric, as for the lining, and stitch it to cover the raw ends on the base of the basket.

7. Cut two 45 x 4cm(18 x 1½in) pieces of silk and two matching pieces of the cotton. Stitch them together in pairs, with right sides together, making narrow seams down the long sides. Turn right sides out and press. Tie them in bows at the base of the basket handles. Turn in and slip stitch the raw ends of the fabric to neaten.

This tiny basket was just asking to be turned into a really special pincushion.

Frilled pincushion

Materials

- Small basket (about 18cm(7in) tall)
- Pink enamel spray paint
- Scraps of pink and mauve shot silk
- Polyester wadding
- Pins
- PVA glue

1. Stand the basket inside an old cardboard box and spray lightly with the pink paint. Give the basket several light coats to cover it completely. Leave to dry.

2. Fill the basket with torn scraps of wadding, pressing it down firmly. Cut a circle of mauve silk about 4cm(1½in) larger than the diameter of the basket. Lay this over the wadding and tuck it down inside the basket. Glue the fabric edges to the wicker work.

3. Cut and join several 5cm(2in) wide pieces of pink silk from along the selvedges. You will need a finished piece long enough to go round the basket about two-and-a-half times. Turn over the raw edge to the wrong side and run a gathering thread near the fold. Pull up the gathers to fit round the top of the basket. Glue to the edge and decorate with pins. Make two small bows from the mauve silk and glue on at the base of the handles.

Hanging basket

Materials

- Round basket, about 20cm(8in) diameter
- 4m(4½yd) floral printed satin ribbon, 2.5cm(1in) wide
- Bondaweb fusible fleece
- PVA glue

1. Cut four pieces of ribbon 54cm(21in) long. Cut two pieces of Bondaweb to the same size. Iron this to the reverse of two of the pieces of ribbon, following the maker's instructions. Peel off the backing paper and iron on the other pieces of ribbon so that you have a double thickness.

2. Glue the ends of these ribbons to the outside of the basket on opposite sides so that you can hang it up. Cut the remaining ribbon into four equal pieces. Tie them into bows and glue in place to cover the ends of the hanging ribbons.

Heart-shaped basket

Materials

- Heart-shaped basket, about 23cm(9in) across
- Toning fabrics in pink and mauve
- 40cm(½yd) narrow lacy edging
- 1m(1yd) narrow pink satin ribbon
- Polyester wadding

1. Draw round the basket onto scrap paper to make a pattern. Cut out four pieces of fabric to this size, two pink and two mauve. Cut two pieces of wadding to the same shape, but slightly smaller, to fit into the base of the basket.

2. Place the two mauve pieces together, right sides facing. Stitch round, close to the edge, leaving a 10cm(4in) gap for turning. Turn right sides out and press. Insert the wadding and hand stitch the opening to neaten. Place inside the basket.

3. Cut a 3cm(1¼in) wide frill piece from the selvedge of the mauve fabric, to fit twice round the heart shape. Gather the raw edge and tack it around one pink heart shape, on the right side, matching up the raw edges. Make this into a padded lid as for the basket liner.

4. Cut out a small heart shape from mauve fabric, stitch this centrally to the top of the lid piece and edge with the lace. Cut the ribbon in half and stitch the two pieces to the back of the lid so that you can tie it to the basket, in a double bow, to complete.

Bow basket

Materials

- Round basket, about 25cm(10in) diameter
- Stiffy fabric stiffener
- PVA glue
- Pink-and-white striped fabric, about 50cm(½yd)
- Pink broderie-anglaise edging, enough to go twice round the basket

1. Measure the height of the side of the basket and cut a strip of the fabric to this width. The length of the piece should be twice the circumference of the basket. Stitch the broderie anglaise to the top edge. Run a line of gathering stitches along the seam and another close to the lower edge. Pull up the gathers so that the fabric fits inside the basket. Stitch to the wicker work along the top edge and glue to the base of the basket.

Flower-printed ribbon makes this the quickest and easiest way to decorate a basket.

2. Make a round liner for the base of the basket as for the heart-shaped liner. Glue in place to cover the raw edges of the fabric lining.

3. Cut a 10 x 90cm(4 x 36in) piece of the fabric. Pour on some of the Stiffy fabric stiffener and spread it over the surface of the fabric evenly. The aim is to get the fabric completely saturated but not dripping with excess liquid. Smooth off any excess but do not squeeze or wring the fabric or you will crease it unnecessarily. Fold the long raw edges of the fabric in, to meet in the middle. Hang this up to dry for about forty-five minutes.

4. When the fabric is slightly tacky, tie it into a bow. Place this on the basket handle and wind the ends round the handle. Cut the ends into points and arrange the bow to an attractive shape. Leave to dry until the fabric is hard.

Cottage garden

patchwork quilt

There is nothing better than fresh flowers, from a cottage garden - you can almost smell the country air! The colours are vivid and thrown together in a seemingly haphazard way and yet they never seem to clash. A multi-coloured log-cabin quilt has the same charming feel to it, but the planning stage is important to get just the right balance of fabrics.

There are several methods for making log-cabin patchwork but this one works particularly well. Its success depends on accurate cutting and stitching, but it is relatively quick to make, as all the stitching can be done on the sewing machine. Each finished patchwork square measures approximately 35cm(14in). So use this measurement to work out how many squares you will need to make the quilt to the size you wish.

Above: Arrange a multicoloured bouquet of garden flowers in a large glass jar, pushing the stems into oasis to hold them in place. Carefully place the whole arrangement inside a rustic basket to complete the country look.

Left: This is a machine-stitched patchwork quilt in the American log-cabin style. The different coloured fabrics are cut into accurate strips and then sewn, in order, round a central square to form one large patch. These patches are all joined and edged, then quilted by hand or machine.

You will need ten different fabrics that blend together (dress-weight cotton fabric is ideal). About half the quantity of this fabric should be in light colours and the other half dark, to make the traditional pattern. Each square should be slightly different in its arrangement and combination of coloured fabric, so between twenty and thirty different patterns is ideal for the whole quilt.

It is possible to buy wadding in large pieces to fit quilts but if you can only buy it in the normal width, cut this into lengths and butt the long edges together to make the necessary shape. Ladder stitch or oversew by hand, on both sides of the wadding, at each join.

Materials

- 10 different cotton fabrics (see above)
- Border fabric, about 25cm(10in) wide
- Plain cotton backing fabric
- Polyester wadding, 113g(4oz) weight
- Quilting thread
- Quilting needle
- Long metal ruler
- Rotary cutter and mat, or sharp scissors

Fig 1 Join the two pieces right sides together

Fig 2 Join the next piece to the right hand side

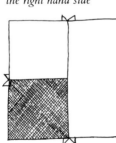

Fig 4 Arrangement of fabric strips to make the patchwork square

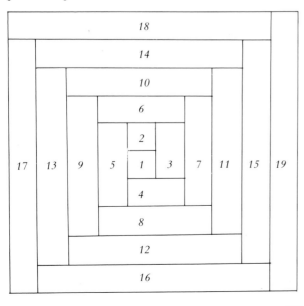

To make one 35cm(14in) patchwork square
(Take accurate 1cm(³⁄₈in) seams throughout)

1. Cut accurate 5.5cm(2¹⁄₈in) wide strips from all the fabrics, using a rotary cutter and a long metal ruler or sharp scissors. Using one light and one dark coloured fabric strip, cut off two 5.5cm(2¹⁄₈in) pieces. Join these, right sides together, taking a 1cm(³⁄₈in) seam. It is important to be really accurate with the seam allowance so that the pieces join up exactly. To help you do this, press a strip of masking tape onto the base plate of your sewing machine exactly 1cm(³⁄₈in) from the needle. Let the raw edges of the fabric follow the edge of the masking tape as you stitch. Press the seam open after stitching.

2. Cut a piece measuring 9cm(3¹⁄₂in) long from the same fabric strip as the light coloured square. Stitch this down the right-hand side of the joined squares as before, and press the seam open (Fig 2).

3. Cut another strip, the same size, from dark fabric and stitch this to the base of the patchwork square, in the same way (Fig 3).

4. Again using the same fabric, cut a piece 13.5cm(5¹⁄₄in) long. Join this to the patchwork, up the left-hand side, to continue the pattern.

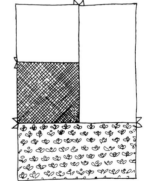

*Fig 3
Stitch a dark strip to the base*

5. Continue in this way, using the diagram as a guide (Fig 4), stitching the strips round the patchwork in a clockwise direction. (Each complete square consists of nineteen separate pieces.) You will see that the length of the strips increases as the patchwork enlarges, so that each new strip is the length of the next side to be stitched. Position the fabrics so that the completed patchwork square is divided diagonally into light and dark.

6. Make up more of the squares in the same way using all the fabrics in different arrangements. You will need thirty-six completed squares to make the king-size quilt, as shown.

To assemble the patchwork squares

1. Stitch the squares together in rows of six so that first the dark sides are next to each other and then the light ones. To make the second row of six squares, join the light sides together first then the dark sides (Fig 5). This means that when you join the rows of squares in this order, the dark areas form distinct diagonal bands across the quilt. This is a traditional design that is known as the Straight Furrow. Press open all the seams on the wrong side.

2. Join all the rows of squares together in order, as described, to make the centre section of your quilt. Tack (baste) them before machine-stitching, to check that they are in the correct positions to form the pattern and also that the seam lines match up accurately. Press all the seams open on the reverse of the patchwork.

3. Cut long 5.5 cm(2¹⁄₈in) wide strips from one of the plainer fabrics, to edge the patchwork. Use the same method as for the patchwork, stitching the strips to each side in turn.

Fig 5 Stitch the squares together in rows, to make the light and dark bands

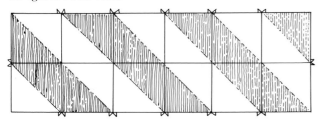

Close-up of the quilt showing the border detail and contrasting backing fabric.

To make up the quilt

1. Cut the border fabric into 25cm(10in) wide strips. Each strip should be 48cm(19¹⁄₄in) longer than the side it will be stitched to. This will give an overlap at the corners, which allows you to make a mitre, so that the border pattern continues around the edge neatly.

2. With right sides together and raw edges matching, stitch the border strips centrally onto each side of the patchwork, taking 1cm(³⁄₈in) seams. Fold the overlapping fabric, at each corner, to a 45 degree angle. Press in place, tack (baste) and top stitch close to the fold (Fig 6). Trim away the excess fabric, from the wrong side, on each corner.

3. Join lengths of the backing fabric together to form a piece the same size as the complete patchwork. Repeat with the wadding if necessary. Pin and tack (baste) the three layers together, with right sides outside and the wadding in between. Make four rows of tacking (basting), ensuring you are going through all the layers, starting from the centre and working out to the corners. Then make several vertical and horizontal rows and lastly one row near the edge, to hold the layers firmly, prior to quilting.

4. Using the quilting thread and a quilting needle, make small running stitches in lines, following the edge of each patchwork square. Make two more lines of quilting, within each square, so that the rows of stitching are two strips apart. This stitching will join the layers together securely and quilt the patchwork. The quilting can also be done on a sewing machine to speed up the process, but the finished result is better when done by hand.

5. Bind the raw edge of the quilt with 5.5cm(2¹⁄₈in) wide strips of toning fabric. Use the log-cabin patchwork method, stitching the strips to the right side of the quilt first. Then turn the raw edges of the binding over to the back of the quilt. Press under a tiny hem and slip stitch neatly to the backing fabric to hide all the raw edges. Lastly remove all the tacking (basting) threads.

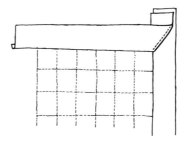

Fig 6 Fold the fabric at each corner and top stitch

Anemone
chain-stitch cushions

Anemones are sturdy little flowers that are inexpensive
to buy and therefore often underestimated.
However, the brilliance of their colours and the
richness of their dark centres make them a most
dramatic and exciting flower. These hand-
embroidered cushions echo the pinks, reds and violets
of the anemones, and feature an easy chain-stitch
pattern taken from Indian paisley designs.

*Above: The brilliant colours of a handful of anemones
are shown off to great effect in this pair of vividly
painted pottery vases.*

*Right: Vibrant anemones go with the swirling patterns
of these hand-embroidered cushions.*

Materials for each cushion

- 50cm(½yd) Zweigart DMC Edinburgh Linen 3217 in cream
- 2 or 3 skeins of DMC stranded cotton (floss): 327, 552, 718, 666, 304, 310, 554, and 3608
- 25mm(1in) squared graph paper
- Fine black waterproof felt-tipped pen
- Soluble embroidery marker pen
- Crewel embroidery needles
- Embroidery frame (optional)
- No3 piping cord, about 1.5m(1½yd)
- Scraps of toning silk to cover piping cord
- Zipper foot for sewing machine
- Matching threads
- Round or square cushion pad, size 38cm(15in)

Above: Anemones need very little added foliage as each stem has its own circle of green fronds just below the bloom. They look their best simply massed together in a colourful bowl. Push the flowers together closely to form a glorious block of colour.

To make the cushion

1. Draw out the pattern onto the graph paper (each square represents one inch (25mm) using the black waterproof felt-tipped pen. Copy the design overleaf, square by square.

2. Cut out a piece of linen to measure 46cm(18in) for both the round and the square cushion. Place this over the paper pattern, so that the complete design will be in the centre, then pin in place all round the edge. Using the soluble marker pen draw in the lines of the pattern onto the linen. Turn the pattern and place it so that the paisley shapes interlock and then trace, as before, to complete the design. Draw in the triangular shapes to fit the square design.

3. Do not divide the stranded cotton (floss), but use all six strands at a time to make a thick row of stitching. Cut it into pieces about 50cm(20in) long to avoid tangling as you sew. Choose a strong colour and, following the chain-stitch diagram (Fig 1), begin stitching the design round the outer line of one of the paisley shapes. You can work in an embroidery frame if you wish.

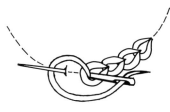

*Fig 1
Chain stitch*

4. Continue stitching the design using a different colour for each complete row or area of the design. You can do both paisley shapes in the same mix of colours or vary them as you wish. Fill in areas so that some of the rows touch as they follow the shapes of the traced design. When you have completed both paisley shapes, work the triangular corner pieces if you are making the square cushion.

Opposite: The square cushion, showing the embroidered triangles in each corner

5. Before you make the embroidery into the cushion cover, press the back of the stitching carefully. Lay it face down onto a piece of clean cotton fabric. Lay another piece of cotton on top and press gently with a steam iron. This method raises the texture of the stitches rather than flattening and distorting them. If the action of embroidering has pulled the fabric out of shape, follow the stretching method described in the daffodil needlepoint design on pages 40-1 before pressing. Cut out the cushion fronts exactly to size: 42cm(16½in) square for the square cushion, 42cm(16½in) circle for the round cushion.

6. Cover your piping cord with 3.5cm(1¼in) wide bias strips of toning silk, joining pieces where necessary. Fold this round the cord and then pin in place. Stitch along close to the cord using a zipper foot. Pin and tack (baste) the covered cord round the edge of the cushion front, on the right side and with raw edges matching. Make rounded corners on the square cushion and snip into the edge of the piping fabric so that it lies flat.

7. Where the ends of the cord meet, pull back the covering fabric and trim the cord exactly to length. Join the raw ends of fabric by hand, with right sides together. Then machine-stitch the piping all round the cushion, close to the cord.

8. Cut out a matching piece of linen for the cushion back. Place this over the cushion front, with right sides facing and raw edges matching. Pin in place and stitch round three sides on the square cushion (Fig 2), and leave a 20cm(8in) gap on the round cushion. Trim any excess fabric from the corners of the square cushion. Cut notches into the seam allowance on the round cushion. Turn the work right sides out, insert the cushion pad and hand stitch the opening to finish.

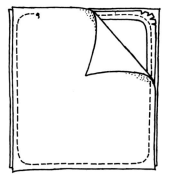

Fig 2
Stitch the cushion-back in place, round three sides

Pattern for half the paisley design (each square represents one inch 25mm)

Ornamental cabbage
hat boxes

Ornamental cabbages are a most unusual and
attractive feature in a garden. Their pink-and-
mauve leaves look wonderful planted among
rose bushes. Their shape and colours made me
think of covering these Edwardian-style hat
boxes to make delightful bedroom accessories.
You can cover ready-made boxes, or make
your own from layers of card as described
overleaf. The cabbages can be used most
effectively in flower arrangements too, as they
have a good stem which can be stripped of
foliage and held in water.

*Above: The cabbages grow in an amazing array of greens
blending to startling pinks and mauves.*

*Opposite: A collection of cardboard hat boxes simply covered in
swirling patterned fabrics and adorned with extravagant ribbon
and fabric bows.*

Materials to make one box
24cm(9½in) diameter

- 1 sheet stiff white card (artist's mounting board)
- 2-3 sheets thin white card
- Large sheets thin white paper
- Spray mount
- Double-sided sticky tape

1. Cut a 24cm(9½in) diameter circle of stiff card for the base of the box, and a piece of thin card 18cm deep x 80cm wide (7 x 32in) for the sides. (You will need to join pieces of the thin card to get the right size. To do this, allow an overlap of about 2.5cm(1in) and fix with double-sided sticky tape.)

2. Using spray mount, cover the thin card with an oversize piece of the white paper, smoothing it with a soft cloth to ensure it is quite flat. Cut the top and side edges of the paper level with the edge of the card, but allow a 2.5cm (1in) overlap along the bottom. Snip this surplus paper into small tabs, about 1cm (³⁄₈in) wide (Fig 1).

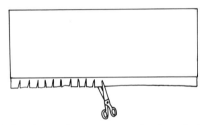

Fig 1 Cut the surplus paper into tabs along the lower edge

3. One-by-one, glue the paper tabs to the underside of the base piece, fitting the lower edge of the sides neatly against the edge of the base until it is completely encircled (Fig 2). Secure the overlap with double-sided tape.

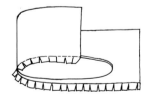

*Fig 2
Glue the paper tabs
round the base piece*

4. To reinforce the box, cut more 18cm(7in) deep pieces across the width of the thin card: join them edge-to-edge, then roll up and place inside, allowing the card to open out so that it fits snugly against the side. Tape in place.

5. To make the lid, cut a 25cm(10in) diameter circle of stiff card and two strips of thin card 6 x 85cm(2¼ x 34in). Cover the stiff card with a 29cm(11½in) diameter circle of white paper, centres matching, using the spray mount. Cut the overlapping paper into V-shaped tabs all round.

6. Glue the paper tabs over the top edge of one strip of thin card to make the sides of the lid (Fig 3). Trim the card overlap to about 2.5cm(1in) and join as for the box base. Spray glue onto the reverse side of the second strip of thin card then stick it neatly round the edge of the lid, to cover the first strip and reinforce it.

Fig 3 Glue the tabs on the circular lid to one long strip

This gorgeous arrangement of fruit, flowers and fabric looks like an old-master painting and would look most impressive piled onto a sideboard or hall table, for a special occasion. Use a large vase or bowl to arrange the flowers and cover it completely with trailing foliage.

Materials to cover the box

- Dress or curtain fabric for the outside of box
- Contrasting fabric for inside box (allow extra fabric for bows etc)
- Large sheets thin white card
- Stiffy fabric stiffener
- Wide wire-edged ribbon
- PVA wood glue
- Spreader

1. Cut a piece of the outside fabric to go round the base of the box, adding 2.5cm(1in) all round for turnings. Spread the outside of the box with an even layer of PVA glue and smooth the fabric in place, all over. Snip into the extra fabric at the top and bottom edges and glue the tabs to the base and inside the top edge of the box to neaten. Cut out a 23cm(9in) diameter circle of plain fabric. Glue this to the underside of the box base.

2. Cover the outside of the lid in the same way with a 37cm(14½in) diameter circle of fabric. Snip the edges of the fabric into tabs and glue them to the sides of the lid. Cut a strip of the same or contrasting fabric to cover the lid sides and glue in place. This piece can be glued flat or use a wider piece and pleat it for a different look. Overlap the ends neatly and glue in place or cover with a bow.

3. To line the box, cut pieces of the thin card to fit inside the base, top and sides exactly. Before gluing in place, cover with your chosen fabric, folding the excess fabric to the back of the card to neaten.

4. To make a fabric bow about 14cm(5½in) wide, cut out a piece of fabric 35 x 15cm(14 x 6in). Pour on some of the Stiffy fabric stiffener and spread it over the surface of the fabric evenly. The aim is to get the fabric completely saturated but not dripping with excess stiffener. Smooth off any excess but do not squeeze or wring the fabric or you will crease it unnecessarily. Fold the long raw edges of the fabric in to meet in the middle. Hang this up to dry for about forty-five minutes (Fig 4).

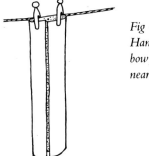

*Fig 4
Hang up the main bow fabric until nearly dry*

5. Then fold the short raw edges of the fabric to meet in the middle. Pinch the centre of the bow and hold in place with a clothes peg to form the bow (Fig 5). Shape the sides with your fingers and leave to dry for about thirty minutes.

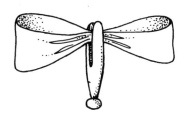

*Fig 5
Pinch the centre of the bow and hold with a clothes peg*

Left: Line the hat boxes with matching or contrasting fabric.

Right: A casual arrangement for the kitchen using fruit and cabbages.

6. Cut a 8cm(3in) square of fabric and soak with the fabric stiffener. Fold to make a 2.5cm(1in) wide strip for the centre of the bow. Remove the clothes peg and wind the strip round the bow overlapping the ends at the back.

7. Make the bow tails using the same width pieces of fabric as for the main part of the bow. Fold as before and then cut in half across the width. Pleat one end of each piece and glue the pleated ends centrally to the back of the bow. Decide on the position of the bow and use PVA glue to attach it to the box whilst the fabric is still slightly pliable. Bend the bow into its final position and leave to dry until the fabric is stiff.

8. For the ribbon bows, tie two long pieces of wire-edged ribbon together with a big bow. Place the bow on the box lid and take the two ends of ribbon across the lid and under the edge (Fig 6). Trim and glue in place. Trim the bow tails at an angle and arrange in attractive folds to complete.

*Fig 6
Tuck the ribbon ends under the lid and glue in place*

$\mathcal{F}$uchsia
deck chair and bag

Fuchsias are perfect flowers to display all summer long in terracotta pots and hanging baskets. They mix well with other flowers, and the trailing varieties are particularly prolific. Finding this lovely fuchsia-patterned fabric (from Laura Ashley) prompted me to make a new luxurious, padded cover for a deck chair, to match pots of flowers in the garden. The tie-on cushion makes the chair extra comfortable and the matching bag is perfect for transporting all the necessities for an afternoon of relaxation in the garden.

Above: Trim off a few branches from a trailing fuchsia and display their delightful hanging flowers in a simple white jug.

Opposite: Relax in peace at the bottom of the garden with this stylish garden seat and accessories.

Materials for the deck chair cover, pillow and bag

- 3.50m(3¾yd) fuchsia-patterned fabric, 120 cm(48in) wide
- 1.60m(1¾yd) polyester wadding, 113g(4oz)
- 50cm(½yd) polyester wadding, 56g(2oz)
- Matching threads
- Hammer and tacks, or staple gun

To make the deck chair cover

1. Remove the old cover and use for a pattern. (If you are making your own pattern, you will notice that the shape should taper slightly at the front of the chair to allow for the narrower front rail.) Lay the pattern onto your fabric so that the design is running in the right direction. Cut a piece of the fabric out, slightly oversize to allow for shrinkage after the quilting.

2. Cut another piece of the fabric and a piece of the thick wadding to match. Place the wadding between the layers of fabric, with right sides outside. Tack (baste) the layers together across the middle several times and round the edge.

3. Following the trellis design on the fabric, make diagonal lines of stitching through all the layers to quilt the cover. If you are using plain fabric, mark diagonal quilting lines lightly with a pencil and ruler about 20cm(8in) apart.

4. Try the cover on the deck chair, trim to fit if necessary, and then zigzag stitch all round the raw edge to neaten.

5. Cut out two 7.5 cm(3in) wide strips of the fabric to fit the long sides of the cover. Bind these sides with the strips, to cover the raw edges.

6. Attach the end of the cover to the front rail of the deck chair, using a hammer and tacks or a staple gun (Fig 1).

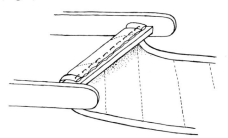

Fig 1 Attach the end of the cover to the front rail

7. Bring the fabric round and over the lower rail, and attach it in the same way to the top rail so that the raw edges are hidden.

To make the pillow

1. Cut out a piece of the fabric and a matching piece of thick wadding 56cm(22in) long by the width of the top of your deck chair. (Ours was 46cm(18in) wide.) Place the wadding behind the fabric, tack (baste) in place and then quilt as for the chair cover.

2. For the ties, cut out four pieces of fabric 16 x 81 cm(6½ x 32in). Fold them in half lengthways, with right sides inside and stitch 1 cm(⅜in) from the long raw edge. Turn right sides out and press. Make a pleat in one end of each piece and pin them in pairs on the right side of one narrow end of the quilted pillow piece (Fig 2).

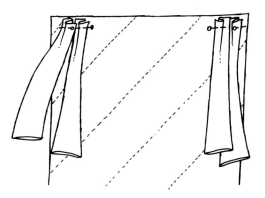

Fig 2 Pin the ties, in pairs, to one end

3. Fold the other end of the quilted fabric over to enclose the ties and stitch along this edge, taking a 1cm(⅜in) seam. Turn right sides out and push in a little more wadding to pad the pillow. Then bind the open ends, as for the sides of the chair cover. Tie in bows onto the deck chair and trim the ties to length. Fold in the raw ends and stitch to neaten.

A roomy beach bag made from padded and quilted cotton fabric. The design incorporates an outer pocket for sunglasses and magazines while the inside is large enough to hold towels and swimsuits. When empty the bag folds flat for packing or storing.

To make the bag

1. Cut out two pieces of the fabric and a piece of the thick wadding 100 x 48cm(39 x 19in). Place the wadding between the layers of fabric, with right sides outside. Tack (baste) the layers together across the middle several times and round the edge. Following the trellis design on the fabric, make criss-cross diagonal lines of stitching through all the layers to quilt.

2. For the pocket, cut out two pieces of fabric and one piece of thin wadding 27 x 24cm(10½ x 9½in). Tack (baste) and quilt these in the same way. Bind the top short end with the same fabric, as for the sides of the chair cover.

3. For the handles, cut two strips of the fabric 13 x 150cm(5 x 59in). Cut out pieces of thin wadding to make up the same length, but half the width, to pad each piece. Fold the fabric in half, along the length, with right sides inside. Lay the wadding in place and stitch the long sides 1cm(³⁄₈in) from the raw edges. Turn right sides out and press lightly. Top stitch down each piece near the long edges.

4. Pin the handles onto the outside of the bag piece so that their ends overlap in the middle which will be the base of the bag, when it is made up. Position the pocket between the handles, on one side, so that the bound top edge is 16.5cm (6½in) down from the short raw edge. Turn the lower edge under and stitch to the bag. Tuck the raw side edges under the handles and tack (baste) in place. Top stitch the handles in position, leaving about 10cm(4in) unstitched at the short ends of the bag (Fig 3). Where the stitching ends it is advisable to make several rows of criss-cross stitching to give added strength. Make sure the pocket sides are also stitched.

5. Now fold the bag in half, with right sides inside, and stitch the sides together taking 1cm(³⁄₈in) seams. Neaten these side seams with zigzag stitch. Flatten the corners of the bag and stitch across the seams, at right angles, about 5cm(2in) down from the point (Fig 4). This squares off the base of the bag to help it stand up. Turn the bag right sides out.

6. To complete, bind the top raw edge of the bag with a 7.5cm(3in) wide strip of the same fabric.

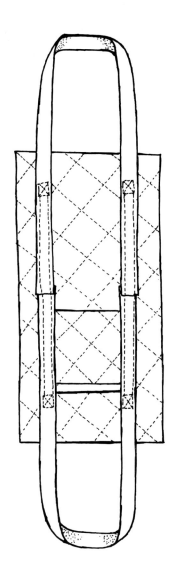

Fig 3 Top stitch the handles to the bag

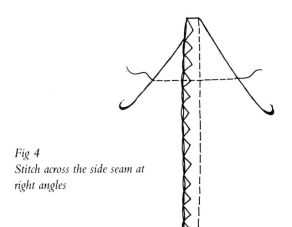

*Fig 4
Stitch across the side seam at
right angles*

Marigold
decorated flower pots

Marigolds are a typical cottage-garden flower. Their sunny faces brighten up even the dingiest corner and they grow happily in containers or flower beds. I love their vivid colour and their strange, unusual scent. Cheap and cheerful terracotta pots are ideal containers for marigolds, and I have decorated some of these with fabric to turn them into a stunning floral display that will last throughout the summer. Bring the pots indoors in winter and arrange them on a window sill to brighten the view.

This process uses a PVA stiffening solution which is spread onto the fabric, moulded round the flower pot then left to dry to a hard finish. Bows and pleated frills can be made to add extra decoration. The stiffening medium is resistant to water but the outside of the pots should not be left standing in water or the fabric will become unstuck eventually. The surface can be covered with several coats of varnish for extra protection.

Above: A ray of sunshine on a brilliant orange marigold conjures up all the heat of a perfect summer day.

Right: Arrange a collection of different sized pots and blooms together, for a multicoloured show of flowers.

Materials

- Stiffy fabric stiffener
- Fabric remnants or off-cuts, including striped
- Flat dish and brush for coating the fabric
- Terracotta flower pots
- PVA glue
- Clothes pegs
- Varnish and brush

To decorate the pots

1. Paint the pot all over with a thin coat of the fabric stiffener and leave to dry. Choose a piece of fabric to wrap right round the pot, with the fabric on the cross (bias). This makes it easier to stretch it to shape without pleats and creases. Trim the fabric roughly to size leaving extra at the top and bottom so that you can tuck the fabric over the edges of the pot for a neat finish (Fig 1).

2. Lay the piece of fabric into the mixing dish and pour on some of the Stiffy fabric stiffener. Spread it evenly over the surface of the fabric with your hands or a brush. The aim is to get the fabric completely saturated but not dripping with excess liquid. Smooth off any excess but do not squeeze or wring the fabric or you will crease it unnecessarily.

3. Lift the fabric from the stiffener and hold it up for a few moments to let any excess drip back into the dish. Now drape it round the flower pot, stretching it slightly to give a good fit. Pay particular attention to the area where the top ledge joins the sides, so that the fabric follows this shape.

4. Overlap the ends of the fabric, where they meet, and trim off any extra fabric to make a neat join. Snip into the excess fabric at the top of the pot and fold the tabs to the inside to neaten (Fig 2). Paint with a little extra glue if necessary.

5. Cut the fabric at the base of the pot in the same way. Fold it under and trim so that the hole in the flower pot is left uncovered. Leave to dry.

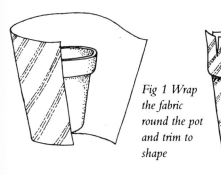

Fig 1 Wrap the fabric round the pot and trim to shape

Fig 2 Cut the extra fabric into tabs and fold them over the edges of the pot

Use bow-decked, fabric-covered flower pots to disguise a simple jar of marigolds picked from the garden.

To make a bow

1. To make a decorative bow for your pot, cut two strips of fabric about twice as long as they are wide. Coat them with the fabric stiffener as before. Remove each piece from the dish and fold the long raw edges of the fabric in, to meet in the middle. Hang them up to dry for about forty-five minutes.

2. When the fabric is slightly tacky, lay one piece onto your work surface, wrong side up, and fold the short ends in to overlap at the back (Fig 3). Pinch the centre of the bow and hold in place with a clothes peg to form the bow. Leave it to dry a little more. You can hold the sides of the bow in shape with rolled pieces of tissue paper until it becomes stiffer and holds its own shape.

Fig 3 Fold the short ends to overlap at the back

3. Meanwhile, cut a small strip of fabric for the centre knot of the bow and cover with the stiffener. Fold the ends in and remove the clothes peg from the bow. Wind the fabric round the centre, overlapping the ends at the back.

4. For the tails of the bow, use the second folded strip of fabric. Pinch the centre and fold it at right angles, then place it behind the bow. Arrange the tails and trim the ends at an angle or to a 'V' shape.

5. Place the bow onto the pot while it is still slightly pliable. so that you can bend it round to fit the curve. Put a dab of PVA glue in several places on the back of the bow and glue it in position. Leave to dry until hard.

To make the pleated frill

1. Using striped fabric is a very easy way to make regular pleats. Cut a long strip of the fabric about 5cm(2in) wide, with the stripes running from top to bottom. Dip the fabric in the stiffener and hang up to dry as for the bow.

2. Using the stripes as a guide, pleat the fabric all the way along to fit round the top of your flower pot (Fig 4). Hold the pleats in place with pegs until the stiffener is nearly dry.

3. Remove the pegs and glue the frill round the pot, a little way down from the top edge. Fold a piece of the same fabric into a narrow band, with the stripe running lengthways. Stiffen it and glue it over the top edge of the frill, to neaten. Trim away any extra fabric.

Choose rich coloured fabrics to cover the flower pots.

Fig 4 Pleat the fabric strip

To make the cut-out motifs

1. Choose a fabric with bold motifs like butterflies or single flowers. Cut these out roughly and dip the pieces into the fabric stiffener. Lay them out to dry for about forty-five minutes.

2. When the fabric is tacky, use very sharp scissors to cut out the motifs accurately round the edges.

There is no need to turn under the edges as the stiffener stops the fabric from fraying.

3. Now attach the motifs to the pots with PVA glue; pots covered in plain fabric will look best. Don't glue them flat, but encourage them to stand clear of the surface by supporting areas temporarily with tissue paper, until the fabric has dried hard.

Fabric butterflies 'alighting' on a collection of miniature flower pots.

Poppy
gingham picnic set

Vivid wild poppies should really be seen in all their natural glory,
making a surprise splash of colour in a sea of green fields – if
picked, they only last a few hours. Poppies always make me think of
summer picnics from my childhood, and this lasting image made me
decide to design the perfect poppy picnic set. I have chosen fabrics
in check, tartan and spots to blend into a profusion of reds
that make you hungry just to look at them! Empty wicker baskets are
easily obtainable and the instructions give details of measuring and
making a pattern to fit whichever size you choose.

Above: A glorious sea of poppies stretching to the horizon.

*Opposite: My perfect picnic set consists of a traditional wicker hamper
with a padded tartan lining, a red-and-white gingham cloth with
matching napkins and a padded cutlery roll for each person.*

Picnic hamper lining
(hamper approximately 47 x 32cm/18½ x 12in)

Materials

- 1.50m(1¾yd) tartan-patterned dress fabric
- 1m(1yd) red-and-white spotted cotton fabric for binding (this will be enough for several cutlery rolls as well)
- 70cm(¾yd) 113g(4oz) polyester wadding
- Matching threads
- Scrap paper to make a pattern

1. Lay a large piece of paper into the base of the hamper pushing it well into the corners. Press it up the sides making folds and creases to mark the shape of the hamper. Remove the paper and cut off the excess paper so that you have a shape similar to the diagram (Fig 1). Try this in the hamper and cut off or add pieces until you have exactly the right size. Measuring never works quite as well as this method, as the hampers are handmade and may not be exactly square.

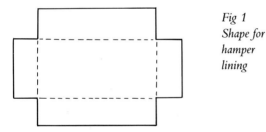

Fig 1
Shape for
hamper
lining

2. Fold the tartan fabric in half and pin the pattern in place. Cut out two pieces, adding about 2cm(¾in) all round to allow for shrinkage after quilting. This can be trimmed later to the exact size. Cut out a piece of the wadding to match. Place the wadding between the layers of fabric, with right sides outside. Tack (baste) the layers together across the middle and round the edge.

3. Machine-stitch across the fabric, in both directions, to quilt it. Use the lines of the tartan to guide you, making a pattern of squares. Try the quilted fabric in the hamper and trim, if necessary, to fit exactly. Zigzag stitch all round the edge.

4. Fold the spotted fabric diagonally and mark and cut it into 5cm(2in) wide bias strips to use for binding. Bind the long edges of the quilted lining with this spotted binding (Fig 2). Cut these ends of the binding level with the raw edge of the fabric.

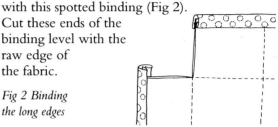

Fig 2 Binding
the long edges

5. Now use 66cm(26in) pieces of binding to neaten the corner pieces. Stitch them in place so that you have equal lengths of binding left at each end. Stitch the end pieces, with right sides inside, to make rouleaus (Fig 3). Then turn each one right sides out and hand stitch the open ends to neaten. Place the lining into the hamper and tie the rouleaus in bows, through the wickerwork, to hold it in place.

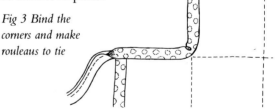

Fig 3 Bind the
corners and make
rouleaus to tie

6. Measure the lid of the hamper and make a quilted and bound piece to line the inside of the lid. Make sure that it does not obscure the method of fastening the basket. Add rouleau-stitched pieces of spotted binding to each corner so that you can tie it in place with little bows.

This shows the ingenious folding cutlery holders that double up as individual picnic place mats. They keep the cutlery clean on the way to the picnic and then you can replace the utensils and tie them up neatly to travel home safely for washing, together with the tie-on basket lining, cloth and napkins.

Traditional terracotta pots make lovely rustic containers for handfuls of wild poppies. Carry them to the countryside in a wide basket and fill the pots with flowers the minute you've picked them. Display them at home in the same basket for a casual supper party or barbecue.

To make each cutlery roll

Materials

- 40cm(½yd) tartan fabric
- 37 x 33cm(15 x 13in) polyester wadding, 113g(4oz)
- Approx 216cm(85in) bias-cut strips of red-and-white spotted fabric, 5cm(2in) wide
- Matching threads

1. Cut out two pieces of the tartan fabric and one piece of wadding to measure 33 x 25cm(13 x 10in). Place the wadding between the layers of fabric, with right sides outside. Tack (baste) the layers together across the middle and round the edge.

2. Cut out two pieces of the tartan fabric and one piece of wadding to measure 33 x 12cm(13 x 4½in). Place the wadding between the layers and tack (baste) as before.

3. Use a piece of the spotted bias binding to bind one long edge of the smaller piece of tartan fabric.

4. Lay the small piece on top of the large piece, matching up the raw edges along the bottom. Pin the pieces together and make five lines of machine-stitching down the fabric to quilt it and make the cutlery compartments, following the diagram (Fig 4).

5. Using a cup or glass and a pencil, draw rounded corners onto the quilted fabric. Zigzag stitch all round, following the raw edge and the pencilled curves, to neaten. Then trim off the excess fabric at the corners, close to the stitching.

6. Bind all round the edges of the fabric with the spotted bias strip. Overlap the ends to neaten.

7. Cut off a 75cm(30in) long piece of the spotted bias strip. Fold it in half lengthways, right sides together, and stitch down the long side 1cm(⅜in) from the raw edge. Using a bodkin, turn right sides out and press to make a rouleau. Fold in and hand stitch the ends to neaten. Hand stitch the centre point of this to the centre back of the quilted cutlery roll, so that when you fold over the sides of the roll, you will be able to tie the strip round it in a bow.

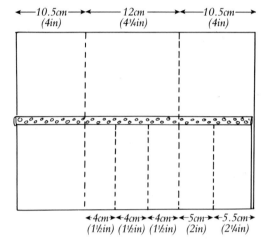

Fig 4 Position of stitching lines on cutlery roll

To make the cloth and napkins

Materials

- 1.40m(1½yd) red-and-white gingham, 115cm(45in) wide
- Matching threads

1. Lay the fabric out flat on your work surface and cut out a square piece, across the complete width, for the cloth. Turn under the raw edges and slipstitch or zigzag stitch to neaten.

2. Cut the remaining fabric into small squares and finish, as for the cloth, to make several matching napkins.

Lily

silk-painted cushions

These gorgeous blooms are not only beautiful to look at but
their scent is quite exquisite. As few as five flowers can fill a whole room
with their delicious perfume. They last well in mixed floral arrangements
and just a few stems can be most impressive on their own. My particular
favourites are these 'Stargazer' lilies with their beautiful pink-striped
centres and rich orange stamens.
The best way to reproduce their shapes and colours was to create a design
to be painted onto silk – the vibrant colours of silk painting seemed the
only way to capture their exotic beauty. The painted fabric can be made
into beautifully luxurious cushions or a gorgeous scarf.

Materials

- White silk crêpe de Chine, about 50cm(½yd) for each cushion
- Pebeo silk paints in plum, poppy red, raspberry, moss green, primary yellow, silver grey, plus thinner
- Tube of Pebeo clear gutta with applicator
- Watercolour brushes
- Fine black waterproof felt-tipped pen
- Silk pins or drawing pins
- Wooden frame for stretching the silk
- Masking tape
- Coarse sea salt
- Backing fabric and wadding to make up the cushion covers
- Cushion pads

*Left: Enlarge a single flower for a stunning cushion design.
Quilt around the lily petals and stamens, then stitch wandering
lines all over the background.*

*Right: Use the complete lily pattern or just choose one large
flowerhead for the centre of your cushion cover. Edge the cover
with contrasting piping or a frill.*

1. Trace the design (opposite) carefully using the black felt-tipped pen (Fig 1). If you wish to enlarge it, draw it out onto graph paper square by square. Each square represents one inch(25mm).

2. Cut out the silk slightly larger than the finished size. Using silk pins, stretch your piece of silk over the wooden frame. Tape the design to the frame, underneath the silk, so that you can see it clearly. If the silk is too thick to see through, work on a glass-topped table, with a light shining underneath. Using a tube of clear gutta with a fine nozzle, draw over the silk following your design lines making sure that all the lines of gutta are solid and joined (Fig 2). If there is a gap, the colours will leak out of one area into the next and spoil the design. Leave the gutta to dry for an hour or two before you begin painting.

Fig 2 Follow the outline of the design with clear gutta

3. Mix up the colours for the design on a selection of old saucers. Try out each shade on scraps of silk before you paint on the finished article. The colours can be diluted with water or thinner for a more pastel effect. A good way of shading the colour is to dampen the silk with a brush dipped in clean water and then paint the colour onto part of the area only. After a few moments, the edge of this brushstroke of colour will fade gradually to white.

4. To make an even colour, load a watercolour brush with paint and place it lightly onto the silk, in the middle of the appropriate area (Fig 3). Allow the colour to creep up to the gutta outline gradually, so as not to overload the fabric and possibly bleed into the adjacent area. If you want to darken any part of the area, put on a few tiny dabs of darker colour in this part, whilst it is still wet. The second coat of colour will slowly seep in and create a subtle shaded effect. To add darker lines or spots, leave the base colour to dry and then use a very fine brush loaded with colour to paint on the details. Paint very lightly so that the lines do not spread.

Fig 3 Place the brush centrally and allow the colour to flow out

5. To make the wonderful swirling textures, sprinkle coarse salt onto the area, while the paint is still very wet. Leave to dry then brush off the salt. Applying two or more shades into the same area and then using salt quickly, makes varied and interesting colour patterns. These are almost impossible to control in degrees of texture but the results are always exciting. Experiment first on scrap fabric to gain confidence.

6. When the whole design is painted, leave it to dry overnight in the frame. Remove the pins the next day and fix the silk paints by ironing on the reverse side of the fabric, following the maker's instructions carefully.

7. After two days, wash the fabric in warm water, leaving it to soak for some minutes to dissolve the lines of gutta. If there are any stubborn areas, rub them gently and soak again. Rinse the fabric and hang it up to dry. When ironed, the silk is ready to be hemmed to make a scarf or made up into cushions following the instructions on pages 68-70. If you wish to quilt the silk, follow the instructions on page 44, quilting round the edge of the lilies, before you make them up into cushions.

Make the textured pattern on the background of the scarf using the salt technique.

Fig 1 Pattern of lilies design (each square represents one inch(25mm))

Lilac
appliqué curtain tie-backs and cloth

Finding a versatile lilac print (Sanderson's 'Abbotsbury') was the starting point for this design. The flowers are printed in small bunches that can easily be cut out and appliquéd onto plain fabric, to use for borders or centre decorations.
Use an iron-on fusible fleece to make cutting out and positioning the fabric flowers really easy, then zigzag stitch round the raw edges to complete. Complement your handiwork with jugs of fresh lilac and natural foliage.
When using lilac in flower arrangements, hammer the ends of their woody stems and stand them in deep water to make the blooms last really well.

Above: Detail of the machine satin stitching that edges the appliquéd fabric. This is carefully cut out after stitching to make the attractive random edge to the top cloth.

Materials for the square cloth and tie-backs

- Lilac fabric, about 2m(2yd)
- Plain toning chintz, about 2m(2yd)
- Cottons to match floral fabric
- Bondaweb iron-on fusible fleece
- Self-adhesive stiffening for tie-back
- Small, sharp scissors
- Copydex glue

To make the cloth

1. Cut out a square piece of plain chintz slightly larger than the required size of your finished top cloth.

2. Roughly cut out lots of whole floral pieces from the patterned fabric. Choose bunches of lilac with some foliage attached, in varying sizes. The important thing to remember is that you need groups of flowers that do not have anything cutting across them to spoil the look of the piece when you have cut it out from the main fabric.

3. Cut pieces of Bondaweb to fit on the reverse side of each of these shapes and iron it in place carefully. Leave the pieces to cool and then cut round the outlines accurately. The stiffness of the paper backing on the Bondaweb makes this much easier than cutting fabric alone.

Right: Stitch pretty curtain tie-backs and cloths to go with floral drapes. Choose a plain chintz in a toning colour and cut out and appliqué parts of the floral fabric to edge the top cloth and decorate the centre of the tie-back.

4. Then start arranging the flowers around the edge of your top cloth. Make a wide linking border of flowers with an interesting outline. Overlap the bunches where necessary to make a varied pattern. When you have finalised the arrangement, pull away the backing paper from a few pieces. Work in small areas and place a clean cloth over the shapes before ironing in position to bond the flower shapes to the cloth. Use a hot iron and press firmly to bond securely. Continue in this way all round the edge of the cloth.

5. Now set your machine to a very close-set zigzag stitch. Try it out on spare fabric until you achieve a satin-stitch effect that you can use to edge the appliquéd pieces, so that the raw edges are covered and the fabric will not fray. Now stitch all round the appliqué on the cloth, changing the colours of the thread to match the colours of the flowers and leaves as you go. Try to overlap the ends of the lines of stitching with the next line so that the

threads are less likely to come unravelled and the finish is neat. Where you cannot do this, pull the threads through to the back of the work and knot them together, before cutting them off.

6. Using the sharp-pointed scissors, trim away the plain fabric around the outside edge of the cloth (Fig 1). Cut very close to the stitching but be careful not to cut the zigzag threads. If this does happen by accident, dab on a tiny amount of Copydex glue on the reverse, to hold the threads. Display this cloth over a long plain cloth in the same or a toning colour.

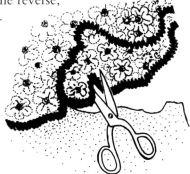

Fig 1 Trim away the plain fabric close to the stitching

To make the tie-backs

1. Draw out the full-sized shape of your finished tie-back (Fig 2). Each square represents 2cm(¾in). Cut out this shape from the stiffening. Lay this onto the plain chintz and draw round it lightly in pencil. Cut out two of these shapes from the chintz, adding 2cm(¾in) all round for seams.

2. Make up some appliqué pieces, as for the cloth, and iron them onto the centre of the tie-back in an attractive arrangement. Sew in place with zigzag stitch, as before, and press. Remove the backing paper and attach the stiffening centrally to the reverse side of the appliquéd fabric.

3. Cut out 10cm(4in) wide pieces of the chintz to make a frill for the tie-back. Join lengths to make a piece about twice the circumference of the tie-back. Fold this in half, along the length, with right sides outside. Run a gathering thread along the length, near the raw edges. Pull up the gathers evenly and pin the frill around the appliquéd tie-back (Fig 3). Stitch in place around the tie-back just outside the stiffening. Press flat so that the frill stands out all round the edge.

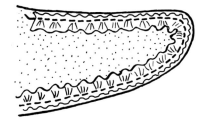

Fig 3 Stitch the frill all round the edge of the tie-back matching up the raw edges

4. Turn in the edges of the other piece of chintz and press to the reverse side. Lay this onto the back of the tie-back, right side out, and slip stitch in place all round, to neaten. Sew a ring to each end of the tie-back to use with wall-mounted hooks.

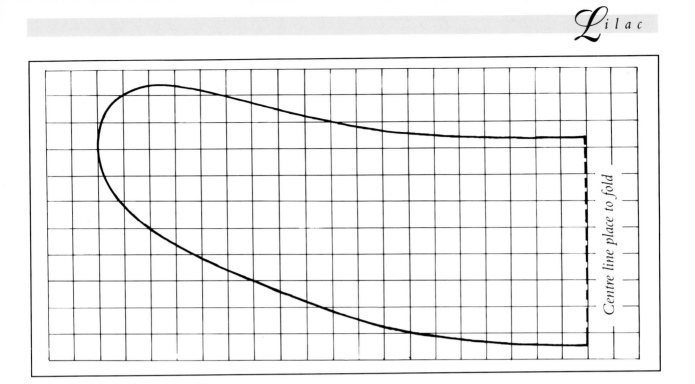

Centre line place to fold

Fig 2 Shape for tie-back (each square represents 2cm ³⁄₄in)

Below: Make a dramatic floral display with several bunches of lilac in toning green jugs. Add a few contrasting sprays of variegated foliage, some matching fabric and a few well-chosen accessories to complete the effect.

Wild flowers

stencilled border

Field and hedgerow flowers are a fast disappearing delight. There used to be a profusion of these flowers each year but extensive building and modern farming methods have all taken their toll. Growing your own wild flowers could be the answer. If your garden is large enough, why not set aside an area to go wild? You can allow resident wild plants to seed themselves naturally and help them along with packets of wild flower seeds to introduce more unusual species.

I like to celebrate the beauty of wild flowers by using them in my designs. This pretty garland stencil combines a selection of my favourite blossoms with romantic ribbon bows. You can stencil this onto painted walls and furniture or even onto fabric, using special washable paints.

In general I would advise people not to pick wild flowers, for by removing them from their natural habitat you are also taking away the seeds that are forming for next year's crop. However, if you grow your own, you can pick some of the flowers, with a clear conscience, for the occasional charming arrangement.

Left: Place the flowers in water as soon as possible after you have picked them, as wild flowers are quite delicate. Arrange them casually in different-sized jars of water and then place the jars into a deep basket. Complete the country look by decorating the handle of the basket with a large bow made from wire-edged taffeta ribbon, arranging the loops and ends into attractive shapes.

Opposite: This two-stage stencil celebrates the delicacy and colour variety of some of my favourite wild flowers. The leaves and stems are cut as one stencil and all the flowers are on the other where you can choose the colours to follow your decor or keep them natural.

Materials for the stencil

- Clear acetate stencil sheet
- Fine black waterproof felt-tipped pen
- Sharp craft knife
- Cutting mat
- Small stencil brushes
- Fast-drying stencil paints in white, red, yellow, blue and several greens
- Low-tack masking tape

To make and print the stencil

1. Following the design overleaf draw it out to full size, square by square, onto graph paper; each square represents one inch(25mm). Trace the foliage and stems onto a sheet of the stencil film, using the felt-tipped pen. Make sure you have about 5cm(2in) of extra sheet all round the edge of the design. On a separate sheet draw all the flowers and ribbons adding dotted register lines to indicate the position of the leaves close to them (Fig 1). This will enable you to position the second stencil sheet really accurately.

Fig 1
Draw in dotted register lines for the leaf positions

2. Cut out the shapes carefully on both stencil sheets using the craft knife and a cutting mat. Take care not to cut across the stencil 'bridges' and thus alter the shapes. If you do make a mistake, turn the stencil over and press on a piece of clear, sticky tape over the cut area. Turn back to the right side and re-cut the stencil correctly.

3. Prepare the wall or bare wood by wiping over with a damp cloth and then lightly marking the position of the design in pencil. Hold up the first stencil and tape it flat in position, using the masking tape. Use guide lines drawn on the stencil to help you keep the design straight for each repeat.

4. Pour a little of the paint into an old saucer and dip the tips of the stencil brush bristles into the paint. Dab off some of the excess onto scrap paper and you are ready to begin stencilling. Holding the brush at right angles to the surface, dab on the paint with a gentle bouncing movement. Make sure the edge of each area is coloured to maintain the shape but don't put on a thick layer of paint or it will look flat and heavy. Check your progress by lifting the stencil occasionally and you will find it is surprising how little paint is needed to hold the design. Mix in other colours subtly to add variety and shading to the stencil design. Leave until dry to the touch.

5. Lift off the first stencil carefully and tape the second stencil sheet in place, lining up the dotted parts with the pattern of leaves on the wall (Fig 2). Stencil the flowers and ribbons in the same way, using a separate brush for each colour.

Fig 2 Line up the dotted lines with the stencilled leaves

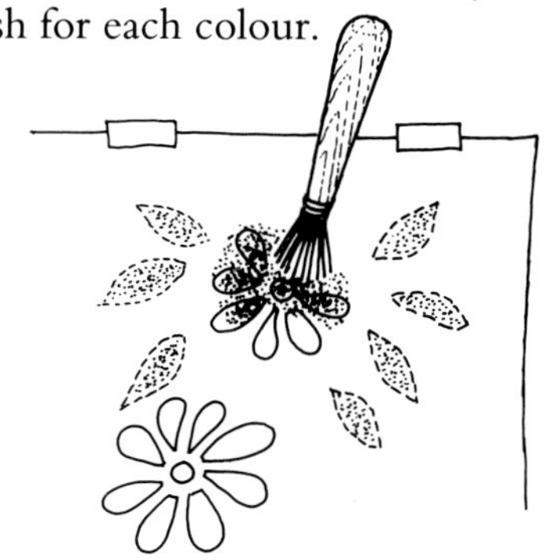

6. When the paint has dried slightly, use a clean brush and a darker coloured paint to add subtle shading to the ribbon, where it twists. This will give a magical 3-D effect and make the ribbon look almost shiny (Fig 3).

Fig 3
Make darker shading where the ribbons twist

7. When stencilling on wood, it is best to protect the stencil with one or two coats of clear varnish once the paint has dried thoroughly.

8. To stencil parts of the design onto matching bed linen, make new, smaller stencils of the parts you wish to use, and follow the instructions for printing on fabric on page 52.

Right: Use small parts of the stencil design to decorate plain bed linen.

Left: Pattern for stencil (each square represents one inch 25mm)

Below: Close-up of the stencil on natural wood.

Herbs
cross-stitch pincushions

Herbs are generally not noted for their flower power but are strong on the scent and texture of their leaves. In Tudor times, particularly, they were grown in very formal gardens with the plants laid out in patterns. These were known as knot gardens, from the intricate twisting designs they formed. Knot gardens were the inspiration for these tiny cross-stitch pincushions. There are three different designs which can be worked into a complementary trio, as featured here, or you could stitch several patterns together on one piece of fabric and make them into a larger cushion cover.

Fresh herbs can be used, tied in little bunches, to make charming decorations. They can also be fashioned into attractive wreaths and garlands to decorate tables for a summer wedding or simply to add a touch of the country to a modern kitchen.

Materials for three pincushions

- Six 15cm(6in) squares of green Aida fabric, 14 threads per inch(25mm)
- DMC stranded cotton (floss): 3 skeins of 3345 2 skeins each of 3348, 703 and 3013 1 skein each of 604, 743, 445, 3766 and 209 (you will need one extra skein of any two colours used, to make the cord for each cushion)
- Crewel needles
- Scraps of polyester wadding
- Dried herbs or pot-pourri

Left: Use fresh sprigs of rosemary with some flower heads to make a long-lasting decorative wreath.

Right: Three different cross-stitch designs all following the theme of Tudor knot gardens. Stitch one or all three for a delightful gift. Then make them up as pincushions or tiny decorative pillows, filled with sweet scented herbs.

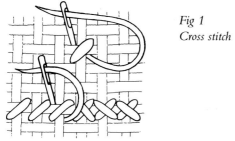

1. Start by making a line of tacking (basting) stitches vertically and horizontally across one square of fabric, to mark the centre. This will help you to position the design correctly.

2. Following the chart, key and stitch diagram for the relevant cushion, work the design in cross stitch (Fig 1). Each square on the chart equals one block of threads on the fabric. Use three strands of stranded cotton (floss) for the stitching. Cut pieces about 50cm(20in) long to avoid tangling as you sew.

Fig 1
Cross stitch

3. Before you make it up, press the embroidery carefully. Lay it face down onto a piece of clean cotton fabric. Lay a similar piece on top and press lightly with a steam iron so that the stitches are not distorted.

4. Lay the other square of fabric over the embroidery, with right sides together. Tack (baste) all round the edge. Now stitch round three sides taking a 13mm(½in) seam.

5. Trim away the fabric across the corners and turn right side out. Fill the opening with polyester wadding or a mixture of wadding and dried herbs

of your choice. Lemon verbena is a lovely fresh scent or try traditional lavender or a sleep herb mixture. Finally, hand stitch the opening to neaten, leaving a tiny gap to insert the cord ends later.

6. Finish off the little cushions with twisted cord made from matching stranded cotton (floss). To make the cord for one cushion, you will need two people and two pieces of different coloured stranded cotton (floss) 4m(4½yd) long. Fold each piece in half and then half again, knot the free ends together. Give one knot to each person to hold and tie all the folded ends together in the middle. Let each person twist in a clockwise direction until the cotton is quite tight. Then bring the outer knots together whilst holding the central knot with the other hand. Tie the ends together and smooth down the cord until the twisting is even. To prevent your cord becoming unravelled when you cut it, wind a piece of cotton tightly round the cord and tie securely before you trim it to length.

7. Using matching stranded cotton (floss), hand stitch the cord to the edge of the cushion. Make a twisted loop at each corner for decoration. Push the ends of the cord into the seam line and finish off securely (Fig 2).

Fig 2
Loop the cord at the corner and tuck the ends inside the opening

Use fresh greens and subtle pink and mauve for a spring-time look.

Colour chart and key for the herb pincushion.

KEY

3345

3013

3348

703

504

3766

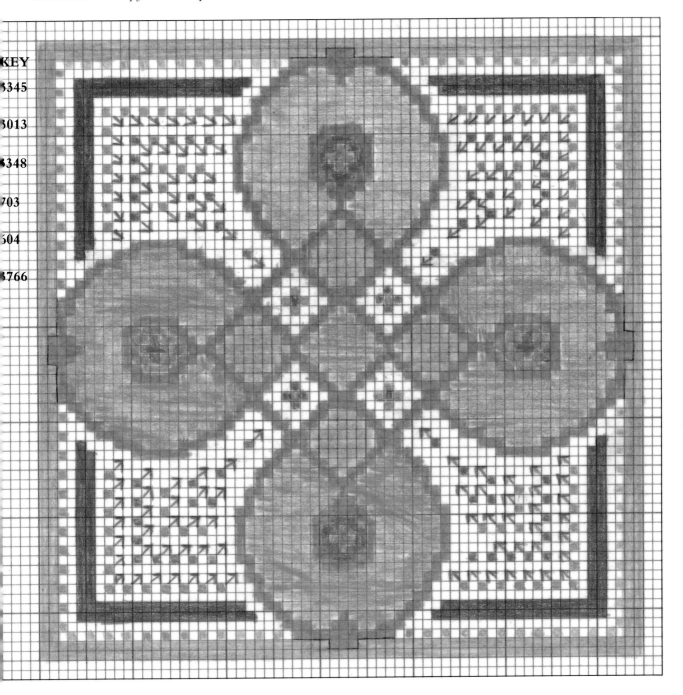

Colour chart and key for the herb pincushion.

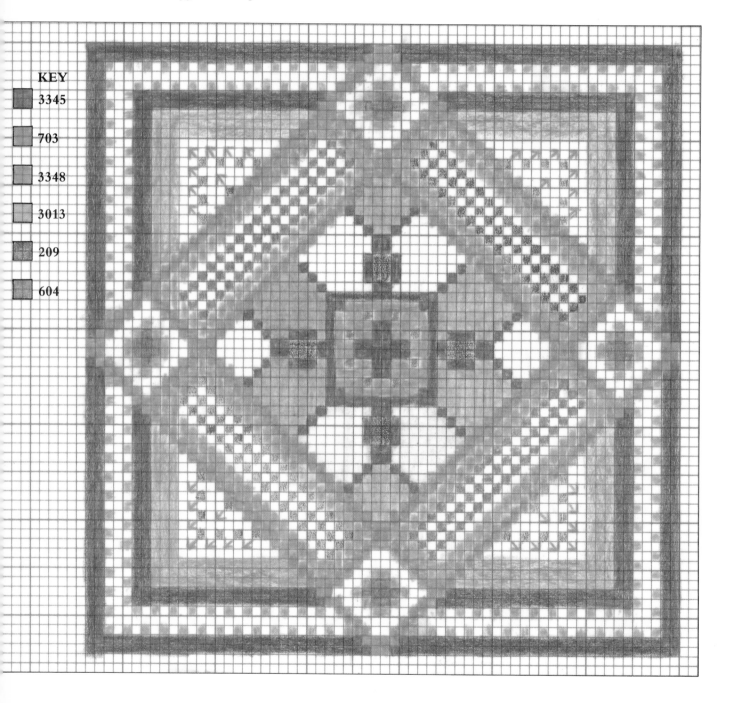

Colour chart and key for the herb pincushion.

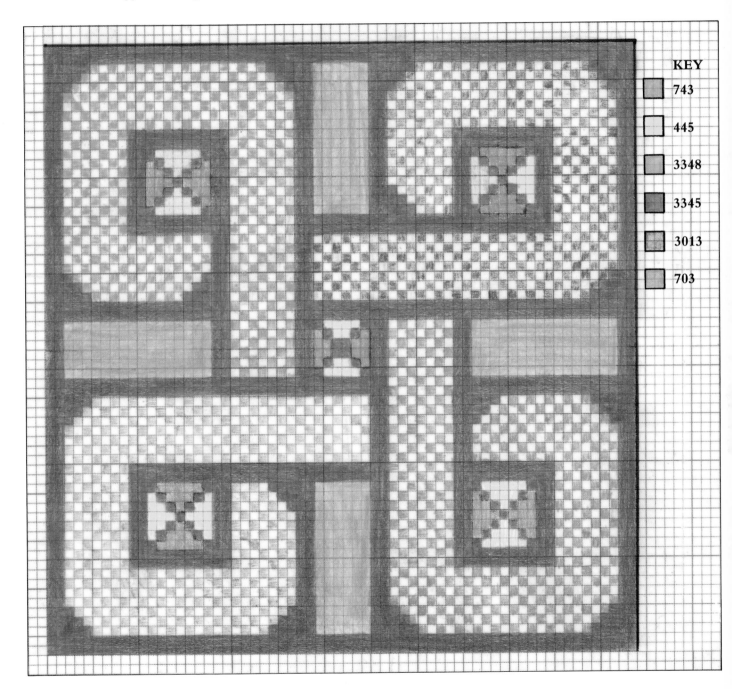

KEY

743

445

3348

3345

3013

703

Garden roses
decorated hats

Summer is at its best when the garden is full of roses, so nothing could be more appropriate for a special summer occasion than a pretty rose-covered hat. Choose a basic hat that suits your face and the outfit, then decorate it freely with fresh or silk roses mixed with fabric and ribbon. You can pin, stitch or glue these decorations in place so that they are as permanent, or temporary, as you wish.

Roses are easy to grow and are excellent for picking and arranging, either by themselves or with other flowers. Their delicious scents and colours all combine beautifully to make a truly romantic setting, indoors or out.

Left: What could be nicer than wandering down the garden with a basket and some secateurs to collect the perfect bouquet of roses?

Right: Decorating a plain straw hat with roses, both real and silk, is a simple yet stunning way of rising to the occasion of a summer wedding.

Materials

- Simple straw hats
- Ribbons in varying widths and colours, including petersham ribbon
- Scraps of silk, taffeta or chintz
- PVA glue and spreader
- Fresh and silk flowers
- Needle and strong thread
- Tiny safety pins

To decorate the yellow hat

1. Start by selecting the ribbon that will go with the hat and your outfit. Choose fairly wide, matching petersham ribbon to encircle the crown of the hat and narrower ribbon to edge the brim.

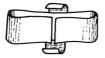

Fig 1
Making a bow from petersham ribbon

2. Begin decorating the hat with a piece of ribbon to fit round the crown. Cut the piece, adding a little extra for turnings. Fit it round the crown, turn in the raw end and glue it to the back of the hat, lightly. Make a flat bow out of the same ribbon with a narrower piece for the centre (Fig 1). Glue this over the join in the ribbon encircling the crown.

3. Tack (baste) narrow petersham round the edge of the hat brim (Fig 2). Fold it over to enclose the edge of the straw and machine-stitch in place all round. Spread a little glue on the raw end to stop it from fraying.

Fig 2
Binding the edge of the hat brim

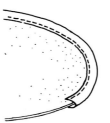

4. Arrange a selection of matching flowers and leaves onto the front and sides of the hat, leaving the bow showing. You can mix fresh and silk flowers on the same hat for a really opulent look. Fresh roses will probably last for about four or five hours if you keep the hat out of direct sunlight. Glue silk flowers in place, or use tiny safety pins to attach fresh flowers at the last minute.

To decorate the pink hat

1. Cut a piece of silk, taffeta or chintz fabric to decorate the brim of the hat and to go with your outfit. It should measure about 18cm(7in) wide and at least 25cm(10in) longer than the measurement round the crown of the hat. Press under the long raw edges and spread a tiny amount of glue along each hem to hold them invisibly in place.

2. Place the fabric round the brim of the hat near the crown, and glue one short end in position, where it will be covered by flowers later. Gently ruche and pleat the fabric so that it forms soft shapes (Fig 3). Spread a dab of glue in several places to hold the fabric to the hat. Glue the fabric lightly where it overlaps.

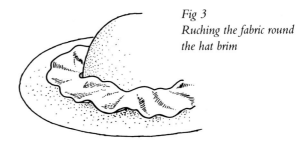

Fig 3
Ruching the fabric round the hat brim

3. Glue or pin on fresh or silk flowers and foliage to cover the fabric join, as for the yellow hat.

To decorate the natural straw hat with multi-coloured flowers

1. Position several silk flowers onto the front of the hat and glue firmly in place. Choose colours to go with your dress.

2. Just before wearing the hat, tuck a few sprigs of fresh roses in with the silk flowers, pinning them in place, where necessary.

Mix roses with a profusion of other garden flowers and arrange them in a container hidden by a rustic basket. The roses last a surprisingly long time if you crush the base of the stems before arranging them and you keep the container well topped-up with water every day.

Holly and ivy
cross stitch for Christmas

Holly and ivy immediately suggest Christmas,
so here are some tiny cross-stitch embroideries as Christmas tree
decorations, either in the shape of a star or a tiny diamond-shaped
sweetie bag. The whole room has been decorated following the rustic
theme, with sprigs of holly strategically placed and natural lengths of ivy
draped casually over the mantelpiece.

*Above: Close-up of the tree decorations, showing the ribbon
bows and the tiny bags filled with wrapped sweets. You could
also make the embroideries into rather special Christmas cards or
stitch the designs onto white linen for a beautiful Christmas
table setting.*

*Opposite: A real Christmas tree decorated with hand-
embroidered cross-stitch motifs in the Scandinavian style.*

Cross stitch is one of the simplest stitches to master.
The main rule to remember is that the top half of
the stitch should always lie in the same direction.
This helps to keep it neat and allows your eye to
see past the stitches to the pattern they have
created. Follow the step-by-step stitch diagrams to
help you achieve the perfect result.

The fabric chosen is especially woven for cross
stitch and is called Aida. It consists of a grid of tiny
woven blocks interspersed with holes, making the
counting of the pattern very easy, particularly for a
beginner. It comes in various sizes and colours and
is an attractive and easy fabric to use.

The background of a cross-stitch piece is not
usually embroidered, so that once you have worked
the design, the piece is ready to be made up into
the finished article.

Materials for the decorations

- DMC stranded cotton (floss):
  666, 986, 3364 for the holly motif
  3363, 3013, 420 for the ivy motif
- Crewel needle
- 50cm(½yd) white Aida fabric, 14 threads per
  inch(25mm) (makes about 28 decorations)
- Embroidery ring (optional)
- Narrow satin ribbon with picot edge in red,
  green and white for loops
- Thin red and green card
- PVA glue and spreader
- Craft knife and scissors
- Scraps of thick card
- Metal ruler and pair of compasses
- Tracing paper
- Cutting mat

For the embroidery

1. Cut out several pieces of Aida fabric about 12.5cm(5in) square. If you are going to work in an embroidery ring use the fabric in one large piece and move the ring so that the fabric is not wasted.

2. Following the charts overleaf and the stitch diagram (Fig 1), embroider the holly and ivy motifs in cross stitch. Use the colour keys to choose the correct shade for each area. Use three strands of stranded cotton (floss) for the stitching. Cut pieces about 50cm(20in) long to avoid tangling as you sew.

3. When you have completed the stitching, press the back of the embroidery carefully. Lay it face down onto a piece of clean cotton fabric. Lay another piece of cotton on top and press gently with a steam iron. This method raises the texture of the stitches rather than flattening and distorting them.

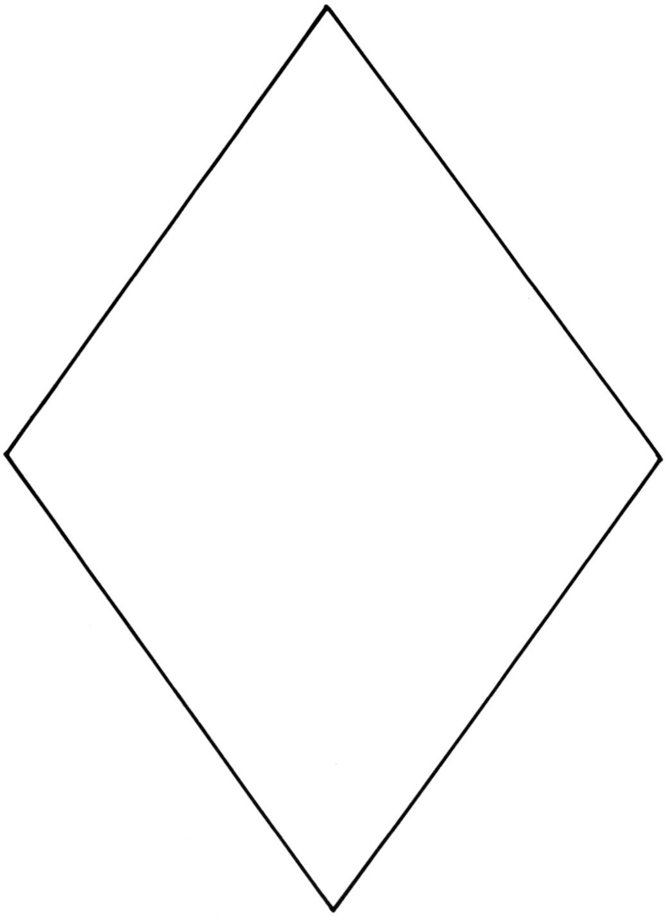

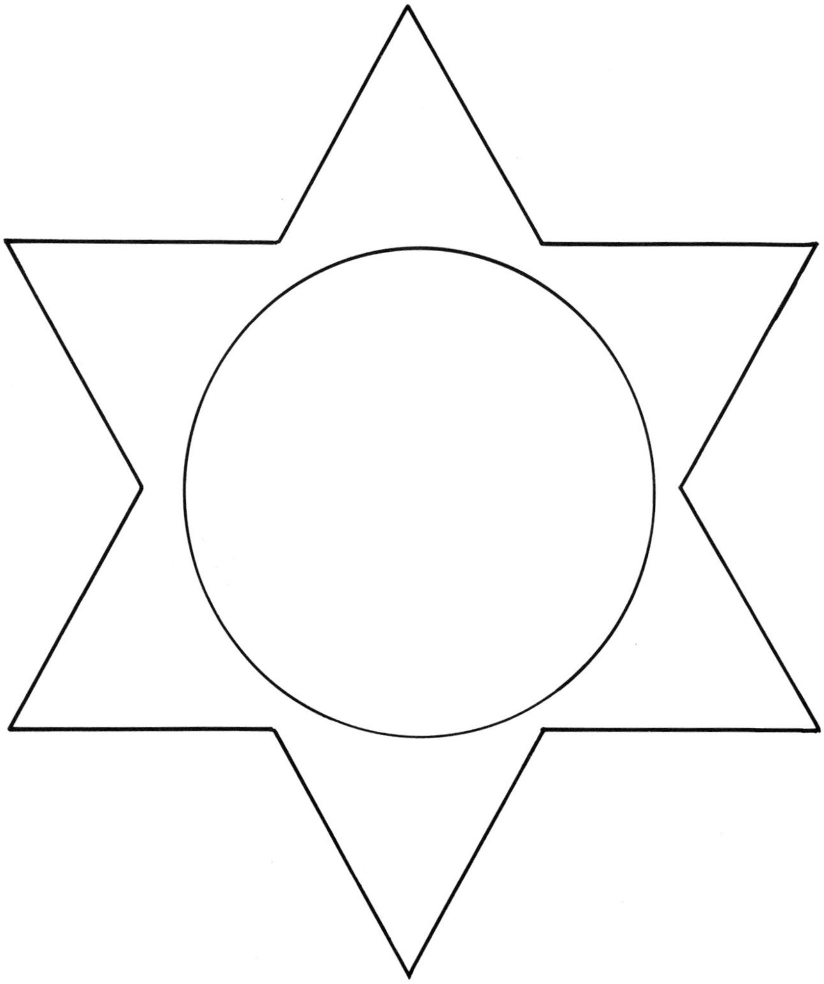

Fig 2
Same-size patterns for diamond and star templates

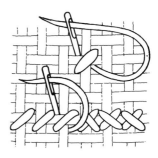

Fig 1 Cross stitch

To make the decorations

1. To make the star decoration, trace off the star shape from the opposite page and cut it out in thick card to make a template. Use this to draw round and cut out a star in red card. Spread the back with PVA glue and place this centrally over one of the motifs so that the design is correctly positioned in the circle. Smooth the fabric onto the back of the card and trim roughly to shape. Glue another piece of red card behind the fabric to enclose it. Leave to dry.

2. Using the metal ruler and craft knife, cut through the layers of fabric and card, round the edge of the star shape. Glue on a loop of ribbon for hanging and make a tiny bow shape to cover the ends of the loop, using ribbon and embroidery cotton.

3. To make the diamond-shaped bag, trace the diamond shape from the opposite page and cut it out in thick card to make a template. Place this centrally over a motif and draw round lightly to mark the shape. Cut this out and another piece to match, from plain Aida fabric.

4. Place the pieces right sides together and stitch the two lower sides, making a tiny seam. To neaten, fold back the top two edges on the wrong side and hold with a little PVA glue (Fig 3). Trim any excess fabric from the point. Turn the bag right side out and leave the glue to dry.

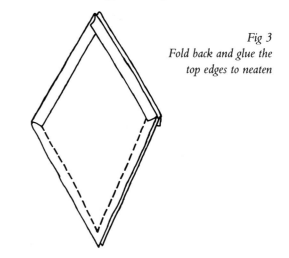

Fig 3
Fold back and glue the
top edges to neaten

5. Glue a loop of ribbon to the outside of the top two corners of the diamond so that you can hang up the bag. Cover the ends of the loops with tiny bows, as for the stars.

Holly and ivy form a lovely decoration on their own for a country look.

Squared patterns for holly and ivy designs. Each square represents one block of threads on the fabric.

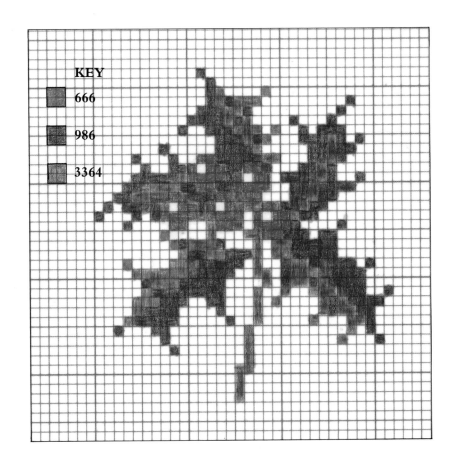

KEY

666

986

3364

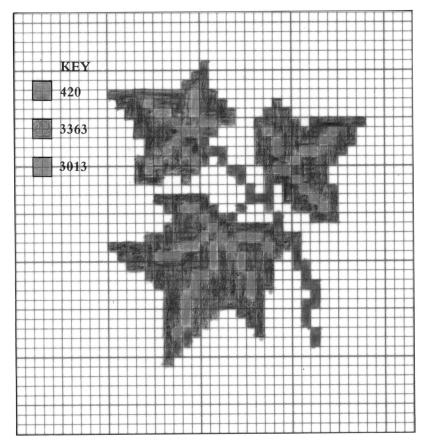

KEY

420

3363

3013

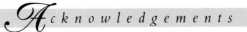

Acknowledgements

*I would like to thank the following people and companies
for their help in making this book possible and also pleasurable.*

Di Lewis for the inspiration of her imaginative and beautiful flower photography which gave us the original idea for this joint effort, and for her hard work, friendship and flair whilst working on the project together.

The expert needlewomen who worked so hard, stitching several of my designs: Sue Robinson, Alison Wheaton and Beverley Jessett.

Kirsty and Kevin and Polly for kindly allowing us to photograph in their lovely homes.

Appleton Bros Ltd, Thames Works, Church Street, Chiswick, London W4 2PE, Tel: 081 994 0711, for supplying the tapestry wools (yarns) used in the daffodil needlepoint. **USA**: Access Discount Commodities, P O Box 156, Simpsonville, Maryland 21150; Chaparral, 3701 West Alabama, Suite 370, Houston, Texas 79015; Louise's Needlework, 45 N. High St., Dublin, Ohio 43017; Needlepoint Inc., 251 Post St., 2nd Floor, San Francisco, Ca. 94108; Needle Works Ltd, 4041 Tulane Ave., New Orleans, La. 70119; Princess and the Pea, 1922 Parminter St., Middleton, Wisconsin 53562. **Australia**: Altamira, 34 Murphy St., South Yarra, Melbourne 3141; P.L. Stonewall & Co. Pty. Ltd (Flag Division), 52 Erskine St., Sydney.

DMC Creative World Ltd, Pullman Road, Wigston, Leicester LE18 2DY, Tel: 0533 811040, for supplying all the embroidery threads, tapestry wools (yarns) for the peony project and embroidery fabrics used in the book. **USA**: The DMC Corporation, Port Kearny, Building 10, South Kearny, NJ 07032, Tel: 201 589 0606. **Australia**: DMC Needlecraft Pty Ltd, PO Box 317, Earlswood, NSW, Tel: 612 5593 088.

C. M. Offray & Son Inc., Ashbury, Roscrea, County Tipperary, Ireland, Tel: 071 631 3685 for customer services, for supplying ribbons for several projects throughout the book. **USA**: C.M.Offray, 857 Willow Circle, Hagerstown, Maryland 21740, Tel: 301 739 6314. **Australia**: Beutron Plastics Australia Ltd, 1 Queen Street, Auburn, NSW 2144, Tel: 02 649 2777.

Nina Campbell for supplying the Tulipa fabric for the tulip dining accessories (pages 42-5). It is available from Osborne and Little, 304 Kings Road, London SW10. **USA**: Wardlaw (Pty) Ltd, 65, Commerce Rd., Stamford, Connecticut 0690. **Australia**: Wardlaw (Pty) Ltd, 230-2, Auburn Rd, Hawthorn, Victoria.

To Gillian Newbery for loaning one of her beautiful log cabin patchwork quilts (page 62). You can order one of these quilts in various designs and sizes by contacting her at Rossmoyne, Barbon, Nr Kirby Lonsdale, Cumbria LA6 2LS, Tel: 05242 76284.

Arthur Sanderson and Sons Ltd, 6 Cavendish Square, London W1M 9HA, Tel: 071 636 7800, for supplying their Abbotsbury fabric featured on pages 94-7. **USA**: Sanderson, 979, 3rd Avenue, New York 10022. **Australia**: Wilson Fabrics and Wallcoverings, PO Box 221, Waterloo 2017 Sydney.)

Laura Ashley Plc, 150 Bath Road, Maidenhead, Berks SL6 4YS, Tel: 0628 39151, for supplying their Fuchsia fabric for the deck chair and bag (pages 78-81). **USA**: Laura Ashley Ltd, 6 St James Avenue, 10th Floor, Boston 02116, Tel: 617 457 6000. **Australia**: Laura Ashley Ltd, 97 Elizabeth Street, Melbourne, Victoria 3000, Tel: 602 2962.

Mary Rose Young for the loan of some of her flowered pottery (pages 54-6) and allowing us to photograph in her house in Gloucestershire. Her pottery is available from The British Craft Department at Liberty, Regent Street, London W1R 6AH, Tel: 071 734 1234.

Vince and Ann of V. and A. Traynor Fine Arts, 5 Oakmede Place, Binfield, Bracknell, Berkshire for all their help with framing various projects for the book.

Philip and Tracey, Tel: 0264 332171, for supplying Pebéo Silk paints.

And of course love and many thanks to my husband David and my two sons, Alistair and Duncan, who have been so patient, helpful and supportive over the past months, whilst the book has been in progress.

We would also like to thank the following companies who kindly loaned items for photography:
Styles Antiques, Hungerford, Berkshire for the silver brush and mirror;
Below Stairs, Hungerford, Berkshire for the French iron cot and garden benches;
Country Pine and Collectables, Devizes, Wiltshire for miscellaneous china;
Original Glory, Devizes, Wiltshire for the gold frames;
Leverton Picture Framers, Hungerford, Berkshire for the gilt-framed mirror.

Index

Numbers in italic indicate illustrations